# I Gotta Crow

# *I Gotta Crow*

## WOMEN, VOICE, AND WRITING

## Jill Hackett

The Writer Books

The Writer Books is an imprint of Kalmbach Trade Press, a division of Kalmbach Publishing Co. These books are distributed to the book trade by Watson-Guptill.

For all other inquiries, including individual orders or details on special quantity discounts for groups or conferences, contact:

Kalmbach Publishing Co.
21027 Crossroads Circle
Waukesha, WI 53187
(800) 533-6644

Visit our website at http://writermag.com
Secure online ordering available

© 2002 Jill Hackett. All rights reserved. This book may not be reproduced in part or in whole without written permission of the publisher, except in the case of brief quotations used in reviews.

Printed in Canada
02 03 04 05 06 07 08 09 10 11   10 9 8 7 6 5 4 3 2 1

Publisher's Cataloging-in-Publication
(Provided by Quality Books, Inc.)
Hackett, Jill.
    I gotta crow : women, voice, and writing / Jill Hackett. — 1st ed.
       p. cm.
    Includes bibliographical references and index.
    ISBN: 0-87116-193-1

    1. Women authors, American—Interviews. 2. Voice in literature. 3. Authors, American—20th century—Interviews. 4. Women and literature—United States—History—20th century. I. Title.

PS 151.H33 2002         810.9'9287
                            QBI02-200124

Cover art © Liz Sivertson
Text design by Chris Long, Mighty Media

Author photograph on back cover by Matt Fifield

# *Acknowledgments*

My deepest thanks to the authors you will meet here, for generously sharing their time, thoughts, and writing experience. Their interviews have been very important to me. I continue to learn from the stories they shared.

Thanks to Elfrieda Abbe, editor of *The Writer* magazine, for seeing something in my query that caught her imagination, and for passing it along to Philip Martin. My thanks and appreciation to Philip Martin, editor of The Writer Books, for his enthusiastic belief in this manuscript, and his thoughtful and patient editing. His vision for this book has inspired me.

This manuscript initially began as my doctoral thesis for Union Institute & University. My Union committee read every word twice, commented often, encouraged much, and has been vitally important to this work. The Union contingent of my committee included Professors Roni Natov and Arthur Jones, and alumnae Linda Tobey, Ph.D., and Ellie Friedland, Ph.D. My advisor Roni Natov is a skilled midwife to writing voice. She understood me when I was not able to be articulate; she can listen beneath the skin and guide gently. Geri DeLuca, Professor at Brooklyn College, gave rich responses to my work. When she responds to writing, it is with the full resonance of her person, and her comments helped me write more clearly. And Sylvia Cowan, Professor at Leslie College and long-time friend, heard in my manuscript when I tried to slink away, and was not present, and when I was in full voice. Sylvia kept reminding me to "Focus, focus!"

Special thanks to Anne Long Fifield and Matthew Fifield, my daughter and son. A writer herself, my daughter Anne did an effective developmental edit on the manuscript and contributed many a lively discussion. She said it was not easy to edit the very person who taught her to speak, but she did it with grace and clarity.

Matthew and I were writing our theses at the same time—his senior thesis for college, mine for my doctorate. We read each other's tomes word for word. Matthew provided empathy and encouragement, and kept me going.

Fellow writer and friend Barbara Donohue is an "instigator" par excellence. She has a knack of getting folks to do what they only dream of doing, and worked her magic for me.

John Stevens listened to me read every word of the initial manuscript out loud, and patiently offered suggestions and encouragement. He gently kept me on track with deadlines.

Mike Fein taught me a lot about technical writing, unerringly insisting on useful content and focusing on the audience's need. He gave me the opportunity to get solid craft skills and learn new authoring tools and media.

Thanks to Miryam Ehrlich Williamson, my National Writer's Union book contract advisor, for her time and expertise in helping me through the legalese.

In addition to those already mentioned, I am blessed with a strong circle of friends, who supported the person behind the project—and through the writing process. Donna Bicchieri provided practical intuition and encouragement. T. Susan Chang shared her publishing experience and warm encouragement. Clare Goodwin's beautiful crow mandala inspired me. Cheryl Lampshire strengthened with wisdom and laughter. Cathy Umphress helped me dream bigger dreams.

I am deeply, deeply grateful to all who have contributed to this work. Thank you.

*Jill Hackett*
*www.jillhackett.com*

This book is lovingly dedicated
to the strong voice and spirit
of my father,
James J. Hackett

# Contents

## ABOUT VOICE

### PREFACE
#### PAGE 13
Structure • Process • Conception • Looking and listening • The authors

### 1: A Circle of Authors
#### PAGE 19
An apprenticeship • Selecting the authors • First introductions • Forming a circle

### 2: Describing Voice
#### PAGE 29
Voice ranges • Three voice centers • Voice and psychology • Voice and silence • Voice and authenticity • Sanctuary vs. vulnerability • Voice in development, over time • Voice as conversation • Physical voice and science • Our map • Now you

### 3: Inherited Voice
#### PAGE 39
Mapping environments • Family environment • First language • Zeitgeist • Blindspots • Early memories • Voice and play • Voice in adolescence • Matriarchal lineage • Now you

## 4: NATURAL ABILITIES
### PAGE 56

Seven intelligences • Linguistic • Logical-mathematical • Interpersonal • Intrapersonal • Musical • Spatial • Kinesthetic • Community • Writer as leader • Listening to ourselves • Now you

## 5: DEVELOPED VOICE
### PAGE 73

The wounded writer • Hiatus from writing • "Separation and individuation" of voice • The athleticism of writing • Discipline • A matter of time • Voice as defense • Motivation • Now you

## 6: CHOOSING VOICE
### PAGE 86

Using emotion • Un-premeditated voice • Choosing identity: "real" writer vs. impostor • Dealing with distortion of perception • The rule of 3 • Integrating voices • Art vs. craft • Thick skin vs. strong core • Allowing for change • Owning our own voice • Not the final word

# THE INTERVIEWS

### Caroline Bird
#### PAGE 101
To hell with the opposition—just go ahead

### Yoko Kawashima Watkins
#### PAGE 113
A shout from the heart

### Phyllis Hoge Thompson
#### PAGE 127
Writing as an act of praise

### Joan Hiatt Harlow
#### PAGE 139
Talent is one thing, and the drive
to express it another

### Carolivia Herron
#### PAGE 151
Looking out on multiplicity
and choosing

### Jill Hackett
#### PAGE 167
Not writing alone

### Louise M. Wisechild
#### PAGE 175
The "I must write" voice

### Regina Barreca
PAGE 187
Speak in tongues, then find your own voice

### Megan LeBoutillier
PAGE 199
I write the books I need to read

### Rachel Vail
PAGE 213
Permission not to have to be Mozart

### Montana Miller
PAGE 231
Life as an opportunity to make a good story

### Appendix One: Selected Books by Authors Interviewed
PAGE 245

### Appendix Two: Bibliography of Reference Works
PAGE 251

### Appendix Three: Credits
PAGE 256

### Index of Authors' Themes
PAGE 258

# *Preface*

ELLIE FRIEDLAND, MY CREATIVE CATALYST FRIEND, SAYS ONE OF THE problems she has when she begins writing is that she never knows where the beginning is. Where she needs to begin may not be where the piece needs to begin, the entrance queue for the reader. But she writes what comes first, then later figures out which piece it is, and where it goes. Like a good Escher puzzle, it folds back on itself.

### STRUCTURE

As an experienced technical writer, for me creating a technical book is now relatively easy. I make a blueprint, sink the foundations for the chapters into my computer, put in the steel girders for structure, pull out my rivet gun and pound away. This piece goes here, that there. When lost, or after a distracting lunch break, I refer to the blueprints and carry on.

This book isn't that kind of book. It can't be built that way. It doesn't use the same hardware, linear logic, or laws of gravity. My raw building materials are not steel and alloys melded together for maximum strength. Instead, I have a cup of tears here, a towel filled with sweat right next to it. Over there is a pile of feathers. Here's a box of dreams, and some books written with colored pencils and tied with ribbons. Stories of lives lived and in the writing. Laughter, applause, scoldings that wound. Rivet guns just won't do. This material is organic, each piece with its own DNA traces. The pieces fit together; there are genetic matches, synchronicities, places where our hearts touch each other.

Geri deLuca, a professor at Brooklyn College, told me, "You never know what you're really going to write until you write it. It changes when you get it on the paper." I've seen this in weaving—all the planning in designing the weft, the graphs, charts, visualizations, and computer software programs cannot ever predict what will come off the loom. In the process of laying in the weft, there is an inevitable "mistake." Like the Hopi Indian potters who make sure they have a "mistake" in their pots to invite Spirit to breathe into them, when we create anything, there is inevitable participation outside ourselves. Call it Murphy, call it the muse, call it chaos theory, God, or angels. Inevitably, what we intend comes out differently than expected.

## PROCESS

I have felt very pregnant researching and writing this book. I will be talking with a friend about something from the stuff of life, and I will feel the book "kick" within me, taking a wild left turn out of the conversation into this developing body of ideas. Though this process of writing occurs deep within, I want to share the excitement of its development.

Caroline Bird also described the process of writing like a pregnancy. Something takes seed deep in an inner place. Then we writers go about building a nest for this fledgling creation to grow, putting a piece here, taking it out, moving something over, until it feels right. (Caroline keeps a whereto.doc file, for the pieces she knows go into this nest, but she isn't sure just where yet.) When the writing is finished, we can move away from it, knowing the idea has a home and will survive there. The "knowing when it is done."

This has been my experience of writing this book. It has been a very different experience from writing something, like a technical manual, that begins in the head.

This is my first nest book. I watched a young sparrow build a nest in a tree outside my writing window. The bottom kept falling out, until she finally figured out how to hold it all together. She worked incessantly because she had to find a place to lay her eggs safely. The bottom has fallen out of my structure for this piece repeatedly too. Roni Natov, professor at Union Institute & University and a friend and key adviser to this work, has been midwife to my writing. She has coached and encouraged, telling me again to just let the ideas come, let it out.

## CONCEPTION

I began my quest for voice bewailing my technical writer training:

> *I am a technical writer, and have been for 20 years. But as an author I have been a missing person.*
>
> *The mark of a competent technical writer is that she shall have no voice, be seen but not heard in her writing. Just the facts, nothing breathing. If you look hard, you may catch a glimpse of her in the spaces, in the traces of how she has sequenced information and how her mind works. But you should not hear her.*
>
> *I have been trained to write mute.*

I have come to appreciate how much craft my technical writing brings me. Somewhere between the steel girders and the organic piles, I discovered more than a truce—I found a helpful alliance. My technical writer can commandeer the loom, lay in the foundational warp, and sit back to help steer when the inevitable "mistakes" come along. But ultimately, it will be my emerging creative voice that must try to weave the organic materials into a tapestry, making a weft that pleases and informs, and honors the donors of these beautiful yarns.

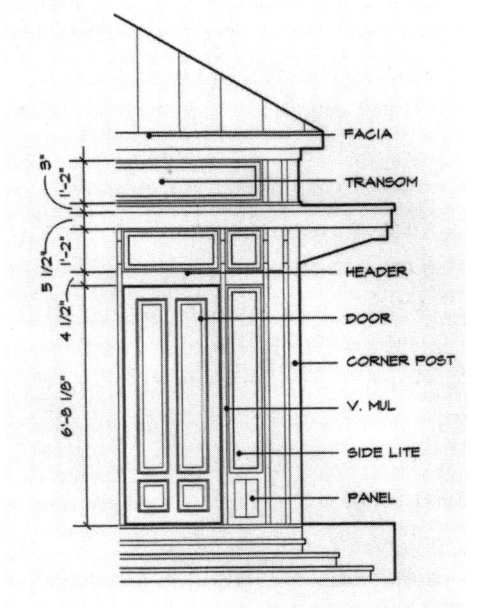

*Blueprint of doorway (Raphael Architects).*

## LOOKING AND LISTENING

Voice is what carries the words—like a signwave (the discernable pattern underneath the words). Voice is the invisible force that directs the communication. To use words to describe voice is a challenge, and impossible to do without using one's own voice in the process.

A Native American Indian once talked to me about his healing tradition, the Orphan Way, which takes not one teacher but many, a patchwork of input. Before he began, he warned me about his words. He said that I needed to listen, looking where the words *point*, not at the words themselves, or I might miss the understanding. And he told me this story:

> *I was walking with a friend one early morning in a marshy area. We were walking along quietly together in silence, listening, looking, a moving meditation. Suddenly I said, "Duck!" and turned to look at my friend. He was facedown on the ground, and I asked him what he was doing. "You said 'duck,' so I did," he replied.*
>
> *Had he been looking where I was pointing, and not just listening to my words, he would have seen the duck I saw take flight.*

As you read, please look behind the words to where they point, and listen to what carries them: the voices of this book. Read the signwaves.

## THE AUTHORS

I want to introduce you to the very special women who offer their stories to us, for this exploration of voice.

I have their pictures all around me as I write this. Their yarns are tucked inside me. I wish I could give you the whole experience of talking with each author. It has been a very special apprenticeship for me. As I write, I hear their voices and their stories in my head, when I get stuck. Now Megan, then Louise, intercedes with encouragement. First Yoko's, then Carolivia's, stories surface to move me on. Rachel's repertoire characters clamor in to watch from time to time; I imagine them peering over my screen seeing how it's coming along. Regina's wit helps me take this all less seriously when it becomes *too important.* Joan's blossoming as a writer, then reblooming helps me defend against my internal infernal critic who is telling me my blooming time is past. Montana reminds me to parse my voice from another's. Caroline spurs me to just get on with it, begin, and keep writing. And Phyllis reminds me to stay fully alive, and to listen to the silences.

But I'm ahead of my story. I have not introduced you to my circle of authors yet.

*Doorway, from the childhood home of Louisa May Alcott.*
*Photo by Terry Barnum.*

# ONE

## *A Circle of Authors*

I NEVER REALLY BOUGHT THAT PETER PAN WAS A BOY. I ALWAYS knew it was really Mary Martin, or Cathy Rigby, willing to lie about her gender so she could fly on Broadway and sing those songs she so clearly loves. Peter Pan is really about girls, for me. Wendy is the lost girl; the actress playing Peter is the pre-adolescent girl who knows what she knows, and isn't afraid to tell you: she's gotta crow.

It's almost as if, at adolescence, we all transition into Wendys. As the boys are all getting deeper voices, we lose ours somewhere. Or it gets harder to speak, or less safe. My childhood ('50s and '60s) had lots of directives, like "girls should be seen and not heard." "If you don't have anything good to say about someone, don't say anything." "If you can't be nice, be quiet." "Be modest, be humble, don't brag." While these are not politically correct statements anymore, their cultural echoes are faintly present just the same. Sociolinguist Deborah Tannen and others are bringing into high relief the ways that women and men are socialized and learn to speak differently: some by directive, some by example and non-verbal teaching.

So, one reason I have studied women's voice in writing is to listen to those who have broken through the sound barrier to be heard. I also did not find many women authors being asked their opinion on these matters in print. Surfing the Internet for anthologies and listings of authors, I discovered that women authors ran about 17% of each list, not the 50% (or higher) which I expected. (Higher, because presently the female population is a bit higher than the male population in the United States.) Tillie Olsen, in her book *Silences,* ranks published women authors at an even lower percentage: one out of twelve, or 8.3%.

Back to Peter Pan, I especially like the song "I've Gotta Crow." It occurs in the musical when Wendy accuses Peter of bragging. Peter retorts that he knows just what he is, and all the marvelous things he can do, and he has every right to be pleased with himself. Peter proceeds to "crow" about his wondrous self, and in the reprise in the show, he teaches Wendy to crow, too.

Of course, the way we have been gender-socialized in this country, it is rare that a little girl would be dressed down for bragging, because it is unlikely that she would. Instead, we are taught early on to be demure and defer. But healthy crowing is a wonderful thing.

And then there are crows, themselves. They hang out in trees and let their needs be known, loudly, clearly, without worrying about how pretty their song is. They just let it rip. They attend to being heard, not to harmony. As women learn to get our voices back, it isn't usually melodious at the git go. We are too loud or inaudible as we squawk and crack. Like the guys did, as their physical voices changed.

Crows are a bit misunderstood and have gotten an unsavory reputation. But they are good caretakers of each other; a sentinel crow watches out while others feed, working to clean up small pieces of our environment. Women with clear opinions who state them forcibly can draw a similar reaction, being misunderstood for the unexpected sounds of their voices.

In 1969 Golda Meir became the first woman prime minister of Israel and the second woman in the world to become a prime minister. In the early 1970s there was a billboard on New England highways of Golda Meir speaking to a large audience. Across the bottom of her twenty-foot photograph it said, "Yes, but can she type?" This billboard stunned me with its disrespect. Perhaps it was meant to be a joke, but no "joke" is without a modicum of truthful intention, otherwise the incongruity that makes us laugh would not be present.

Gaining the fullness of voice may not be a cakewalk, either in attaining it or in owning it. But it sure beats imposed silence.

## AN APPRENTICESHIP

A Chinese philosopher told me that ancient Chinese philosophy believed that the most honorable profession is to teach, and have students. If you cannot teach, then the second most honorable profession is to write, for in this way you may have students at a distance. Though more information is passed between people than can be transmitted on the written page alone, I hoped that by talking directly with authors, I would learn this "something more" and be able to pass it along to you.

One question that I did not ask my authors but several answered anyway is "What book has been most important to you?" For me, Irene Claremont deCastillejo's *Knowing Woman, A Feminine Psychology* came along at a synchronistic time in my life, and resounded in me. DeCastillejo writes lyrically, poetically, with images. Her writing is scholarly, yet with a personable voice. Her first chapter, "On Meeting," explores why sometimes, when we meet someone, we come away refreshed and other times drained. What is this alchemical feeling which passes between people that is not verbal? DeCastillejo describes it as a third presence, a state of grace. My Chinese philosopher friend might describe it as knowledge.

Whatever it is, this "more than words" drew me to interview women authors. I wanted to verbally apprentice myself to their voices, to listen in their physical presence as well as their published one, and to explore together the subject of voice in writing.

## SELECTING THE AUTHORS

I interviewed women authors who have published, whose writing voices have been officially recognized, admitted.

I sought a range of genres, to listen to voice across genre, not just within a genre. I was also looking for new genres for me, and this allowed me to explore these communities of writers. Our authors' genres include memoir, novels, young adult, middle grades, children's literature, poetry, political essays, creative nonfiction, academic, and documentary writing.

I wanted a range of ages of authors, to listen across generations, and across personal development and experience. Our elder is Caroline Bird in her eighties, and our youth is Montana Miller in her twenties. The other authors represent all decades in between. I have roughly ordered the authors' interviews from elder to youth for you, so you can read from mature voice to emerging. I did not ask our authors' ages. Some offered theirs. So the chronological order is not exactly right, but I hope it is close.

The final criterion for selecting authors was that something in the author's work pulled me, resounded in me. I was drawn to each of these women's writing.

I learned that graciousness is by the person, and neither inversely nor directly proportional to their circle of influence. Some I would have expected to have the least amount of time for me richly gave me their full attention.

I feel very honored by the gift of time and sharing of experience that these authors have given. I have indeed learned more by speaking with each of them than I could have learned by reading books alone. I invite you to learn from these authors' stories, and continue the conversation with other authors you know and meet.

### FIRST INTRODUCTIONS

You'll meet the authors throughout the coming chapters, and also in their interviews. I'd like to briefly introduce you to our authors here—keeping it brief because I want you to experience each author in your own way. As you read on, they will be chiming in throughout. You may want to go sit down with a particular author and read her interview in full, and then return to the flow of the chapters.

I'd like to introduce you to:

» CAROLINE BIRD has the longest career of our authors, being our elder in her eighties. I was in the Vassar College rare-books collection researching women authors, and chatting with the librarian about my research. She told me, "You must interview Caroline Bird. She is a treasure." And indeed she is. Ms. Bird's independent thinking contributed important perspectives to the Women's Movement. Her well-researched books include *Lives of Our Own: Secrets of Salty Old Women; The Two-Paycheck Marriage;* and *Born Female.*

» YOKO KAWASHIMA WATKINS came to me through a group of high school teachers (as did Rachel Vail). I was at the Principal's Center at Harvard University, listening to their Distinguished Authors series, and discussed my project with the teachers at my table. They told me, "You must interview Yoko Kawashima Watkins and Rachel Vail. They are such wonderful authors and speakers." Yoko Kawashima Watkins inspires by sharing the experiences she writes about in her riveting autobiographical books. Her family lived in Korea during World War II, and when Japan surrendered, it was a dangerous place for Japanese citizens. Yoko escaped with her brother and sister to Japan. She now lives on Cape Cod, Massachusetts, and travels and lectures widely. A generous and thoughtful correspondent, she has often written me notes in haiku.

» RACHEL VAIL has written a number of books for young adults. Reading them, I was taken right back to junior high, with its angst, high drama, and struggle—and strong friendships. A prolific writer, Rachel was in her late 20s when we interviewed. Her books include *Wonder; Daring to Be Abigail: A Novel;* and *What Are Friends For?* With an avid following of readers, she has a delightful sense of whimsy, interwoven with a solid command of the process of writing.

» PHYLLIS HOGE THOMPSON was introduced to me in the chow hall at Ghost Ranch in Abiquiu, New Mexico. She was there attending a Quaker regional meeting, while I was at a seminar on the effect of place on creativity. I quickly learned that this woman is rich with life. And her poetry blesses her readers with that visceral richness. Phyllis taught poetry for 20 years at the University of Hawaii, Manoa. She has been a scholar-in-residence in Japan, and currently lives in New Mexico.

» JOAN HIATT HARLOW was suggested to me, shyly, by her daughter, Debbie Balas, when Debbie heard I was looking for writers to interview. And I am grateful to Debbie for her recommendation. A teacher of children's writing, Joan Hiatt Harlow is skilled in encouraging fledgling writers. Her own career blossomed earlier, then went through a hiatus, and now it is taking off once again. She writes award-winning stories for early childhood and young adults. Her website is www.joanhiattharlow.com.

» CAROLIVIA HERRON was introduced to me through her book, *Nappy Hair*. I just loved the many voices and its rhythms—it is a delightful read-aloud children's picture book written in African-American praise song. So I tracked Carolivia down through Harvard connections, and met her at her home on the North Shore (she now lives in the D.C. area). Her genre is the epic, and she works with school children to create multi-media, multi-authored stories. She has an impressive range of interests, as her website attests; it can be found at www.carolivia.org.

» MEGAN LEBOUTILLIER was a fellow doctoral student at Union Institute & University (as was Louise Wisechild). My advisor recommended I interview Megan because of her knowledge and interest in the creative process. Her doctoral thesis is titled "Goddesses and Grandmothers." Megan writes creative nonfiction; her books include *Little Miss Perfect* and *"No" Is a Complete Sentence*.

» LOUISE WISECHILD was a fellow writer I met in my entry colloquium at the beginning of our Ph.D. programs. I was impressed by how she takes a stand on issues powerfully and gracefully. Louise has written memoirs on childhood sexual abuse. She studied in Bali during the Union program, and is now writing political commentary from her home in the Pacific Northwest.

» REGINA BARRECA has a website titled "Untamed and Unabashed"— which can also describe her. And for anyone reading her books, or hearing her speak, her creative moxie is contagious. Regina was a keynote speaker at The Humor Project's annual conference, where a friend heard her speak, and told me I must interview her. Regina teaches at the University of Connecticut at Storrs, just down the road from me, so I arranged to meet her in her office. An amazing experience, her office is plastered with memorabilia, notes, pictures, letters; it is one giant collage. I was initially shocked at the disarray—and then inspired to go home and be a bit more "untamed," in the service of creativity. Believe me, it helped me write! Her website is www.ginabarreca.com.

» MONTANA MILLER is our youngest author, interviewed at age 24. I knew Montana as a friend of my daughter's in high school. After high school, Montana joined the circus in France as a trapeze artist, and co-wrote a book with her mother on her experiences. She was among the first women to dive off the cliffs of Acapulco, Mexico, into the wild Pacific—previously a rite reserved only for men. Montana also helped me transcribe all these interviews while she was waiting to hear from UCLA, where she is now finishing her Ph.D. in Folklore and Mythology. She continues to write and perform her stories from the trapeze. Her work can be found on her website, www.montanamiller.com.

» And then there is JILL HACKETT, that's me. You'll meet me a lot through these pages, so I won't go on much here. For the second part of this book, I was interviewed by a friend and adviser from Union Institute & University, Roni Natov. I have been a technical writer for over 20 years, writing many technical manuals, presenting papers and workshops at technical writing conferences (national and international), and writing occasional newspaper articles. My website is at www.jillhackett.com.

Each author brings something unique to the subject of voice in writing. Pictures of each author are found at the end of each interview, so that you might put a face to the voice. And at the end of this book, you will find an appendix listing many of their published works. Many of these authors also include examples of their work on their websites.

## FORMING A CIRCLE

As I interviewed these women and edited their transcripts over and over again, working with their words and voice, they became an inner circle of voices for me. I've listened to their words—thought, imagined, and experienced these women—until I can hear their words inside me as I write. They are my inner writer's circle.

I worked on absorbing these autonomous women's voices, with the wisdom and experience they shared with me, until I felt the processed voices become alive and independent in me.

> . . . *A circle of women is a place where you listen to another woman's truth, and it mirrors back who you are; it's a safe place where women find their own voice and courage; where true emotion expressed by one, facilitates access for others; a safe place for repressed and undeveloped selves to emerge. [Bolen, quoted in Rountree, p. 212]*

I did not expect to be as moved as I was by the stories I heard. I did not expect these women to trust me with the stories they did. The richness of information I received was unexpected.

After a while, the interviews began to "cross talk." You will hear some of it as you read. As the interviews mounted in numbers, I almost did not have to ask the questions anymore. The authors just began answering them, which was surprising to me. And then, something brought up in one interview would be picked up in the next.

As the circle completed, the authors virtually began talking to each other. They certainly were in conversation inside my head. So I present their voices here, hoping that you also will feel part of this circle.

The circle image was so strong for me that I wanted a visualization to pass along to you, so I asked artist Clare Goodwin to create the crow mandala seen on the next page. Mandala is a Sanskrit word that means "healing circle" or "whole world." Clare works ceremoniously, meditating on the intention of each piece; she created this mandala with the intention to help women find their writing voice.

We'll begin our conversation by *Describing voice*, hearing definitions of voice from our authors and others. Then we'll look at *Inherited voice*, examining our earliest patterns set in place before we had autonomy. In *Natural abilities*, we look at the natural intelligences and talents that color voice. *Developed voice* looks at what we do with what we are given. And finally, *Choosing voice* is about when we choose to speak out—and how.

I hope that as you read my chapters and our interviews, and then go and read our authors' books and stories, you also will begin to know these women—that their voices begin to support *your* writing too, and you join the circle.

Let's begin.

*Illustration by Clare Goodwin.*

# TWO

## *Describing Voice*

I began my research with a working definition of voice in writing from Donald Graves and Virginia Stuart:

> *Voice is the imprint of the person on the piece. It is the way in which a writer chooses words, the way in which a writer orders things towards meaning. As writers compose, they leave their fingerprints all over their work. [in Hardymon]*

To this, a potential interviewee responded:

> *By that definition, any writing has voice. Which doesn't mean, of course, that they're worth listening to!*

Exactly so.

Which is one reason why I researched voice in writing. As a technical writer, I have been trained to write in other people's voices, or no voice at all—to erase personality from the piece. So I understand voice by its absence.*

---

* Voiceless writing loses audience quickly, one of several reasons why technical manuals are generally not read, but are only accessed when absolutely needed during emergencies. The "Dummies" series of technical books, however, are one notable exception. There, readers seem to be able to connect to the author's "voice." As the Internet expands, there is a trend towards more personality being invited into technical writing.

When we read something that strikes a chord within us, the voice in this writing is clear, and focused. We understand voice when it is powerfully present, also. The voice of Shakespeare is unmistakable, for instance.

"Voice" is both a noun and a verb. In dictionaries, voice is defined as qualities connected with living creatures: "sounds uttered through the mouth" and "the distinctive range of sounds naturally or characteristically uttered by an individual: *I thought I recognized your voice.*" These definitions [nos. 1 and 2 from the *Random House Dictionary of the English Language;* unabridged] rely on vocal chords.

The action part of the word "voice" is defined as "the right to express one's wish, choice, opinion, etc., or to make it prevail; vote; *as we have a voice in our government.*" [definition no. 7, *Webster's*].

It is also used to suggest a person through which something is "expressed or revealed," as in "the voice of prophecy." This definition is based on a sentient, choosing being, speaking from the authenticity of their experience.

In music, "voice" can suggest a range, a tonality, an intensity, a "color."

National Public Radio did a piece on people's speaking voices. Even played backwards, most well-known people's voices were recognizable: George Burns, Lucille Ball, John F. Kennedy. Can the voiceprints of writing on the page as strongly reveal the author?

Our interviews started with "Please describe your writing voice." Yoko Kawashima Watkins and Regina Barreca answered this way:

*Yoko:*     *In simplicity. A shout from the heart. That's all, nothing more. Tell the truth, and the feelings.*

*Regina:*   *The voice I write in is the voice that I teach in . . . which is a bringing together of a lot of the different parts of my life.*

## VOICE RANGES

When I was recruiting authors, a Canadian freelance writer responded,

> *I'm not sure I have anything to say, let alone anything useful. Voice isn't something I have consciously developed, as I reckon I have one already. And anyway most clients want you to use theirs.*

So she "speaks" in her writing with the voice she is told to use.

Playing with voice, one can write in a falsetto, write "out of one's voice range," write in dialects, write in brogues, throw your voice, imitate, ventriloquize, whisper, shout, be staccato, sing-song, imploring, enraged, seductive, persuasive—all the range of emotions and physical voice.

Writing voice "echoes" within us. Something resounds. Strike a tuning fork and move it closer to, but not touching, a second matching tuning fork. The second fork will begin vibrating, picking up the sound waves from the first tuning fork. A strong writing voice, likewise, moves something within us.

## THREE VOICE CENTERS

I suggest that we have three voice centers: the voice from our head (the rational voice: ideas strike us and set off thoughts and plans), the voice from our hearts (the emotive voice: feelings, memories, longings, and passions), and our body voice (language of the gut, hunches, intuition).

From rational to emotive, there is a range. No writing is purely from one polarity. Technical writers deal with hunches and intuition of how to order their pieces, even while they may strive to erase personality. Poets use the logical-mathematics intelligence of the rational mind to manage meter and form.

Each of us has our primary, favored voice center, but any of the voice centers can lead off effective communication. Each has its own purpose.

## VOICE AND PSYCHOLOGY

As Caroline Bird observes, sometimes a term is just crowning to be born into the vernacular, as "sexism" and "feminism" were in the 1970s. "Voice" was raised to celebrity status in 1982 by psychologist Carol Gilligan's watershed book, *In a Different Voice*.

Interestingly, Gilligan was among the first to introduce a new academic writing voice in this book, hosting scholarly conversations between disciplines not usually integrated: Ibsen responding to Piaget, Chodorow and Kohlberg in conversation with the voices of contemporary girls. Yet among the 153 index entries of *In a Different Voice*, "voice" does not appear. It was not explicitly defined, perhaps because, as our first author said, "we all have one." In her 1993 updated introduction, Gilligan offers:

> *By voice I mean voice. Listen, I will say, thinking that in one sense the answer is simple. And then I will remember how it felt to speak when there was no resonance, how it was when I began writing, how it still is for many people, how it still is for me sometimes. To have a voice is to be human. To have something to say is to be a person. But speaking depends on listening and being heard; it is an intensely relational act.* [Gilligan, xvi]

Gilligan's definition touches on voice in writing: *"how it was when I began writing, how it still is. . . ."* is what we are pursuing. How do you come into your own clear authentic writing voice?

## VOICE AND SILENCE

The 102nd Archbishop of Canterbury, The Right Reverend and Right Honorable Lord Runcie of Cuddesdon, might have debated with Gilligan that *"To have a voice is to be human. To have something to say is to be a person."* In a sermon preached April 13, 1997, at the Memorial Church of Harvard University, the Archbishop said:

*Some of those whose experience is deep are inarticulate. Words can be a rein on the inarticulate. Karl Barth, who wrote thousands of words about God, began each morning in silence, listening to Mozart. Self-emptying is the language of worship.*

Silence is an important language. Not speaking can be an intensely relational act, as is the struggle to find one's true voice. Our voice is shaped by what we do—and do not—voice, and by when we choose to speak and when we choose silence.

The author chooses what is foreground, what is background. Repression is a different kind of silence, and also shapes voice.

The word "communicate" has its roots in two Latin words: *communicare*, which means to impart or share, and *communis*, which means common. So, inherent in this verb is both the action of something going from here to there, imparting from speaker to receiver, and the result of that action, creating common ground, something shared.

"Communicate" also means to have or form a connecting passage, as in "The rooms communicated by means of hallways" [*Random House Dictionary*]. To communicate then is to open channels. A now rare use of the word "communicate" is "to admit to the sacraments of the church; to administer the Eucharist of Communion to" [*Webster's*].

This complements Lord Runcie's words above, underscoring that silence can be a powerful communication as well. To chose silence may still allow "communication" to occur, simply in a quiet form. In fact, the absence of sound may sometimes communicate the loudest opinion.

### VOICE AND AUTHENTICITY

In unknown or stressful situations we often present a false self first, moving later towards the true self, or towards deeper intimacy, towards the more authentic voice, only as safety, confidence, and trust allow. Presenting the authentic voice—even in the privacy of the author/reader visual void—requires inner development of the self and safety.

Authentic voice has the ring of truth, coming from the true self. We know it when we hear it, we know it when we write with it. We speak plainly and from the heart. Yoko's *"A simple shout from the heart."*

We may come into authentic voice all of a sudden. We may lose voice (as our writing voice "cracks"), and later find it again. Or our true voice may emerge after a long silence or hiatus, after the false self has exhausted itself.

### SANCTUARY VS. VULNERABILITY

The false self/false voice can be a shield, a protection as we grow our strength and safety. In many mammals, the throat is the most vulnerable part of the body and is carefully protected as they fight for position. Our emerging clear voices are often tested and tempered by challenge.

This is why I asked our authors about defending their writing voice. Caroline Bird and Louise Wisechild responded in this way:

> Caroline: *I'll defend my ideas, all right. . . . What I have to say, I will certainly defend, and do.*

> Louise: *One of the biggest experiences that comes to mind is when the reviewer for a national gay and lesbian newspaper wrote that I was, essentially, crazy, and that the book was too painful to read. She really blew it off, big time. I was outraged.*
>
> *But I did notice that when there's a direct attack like that, I rise to defend myself. That experience in itself is validating because it made me look for support. . . . At that time, some other people, who I didn't know and who had read my book, came to my defense pretty strongly in their letters.*
>
> *So altogether it turned out to be a really positive experience.*

The element of safety, of sanctuary, is necessary for true writing voice to emerge.

> *Temenos, the Greek word for sanctuary, is what allows truth about who we are, what we feel, and what we have experienced to emerge into consciousness and into spontaneous expression. [Bolen as quoted in Rountree, p. 212]*

We are challenged to develop the toughness of skin to shed criticism and/or to develop the depth of belief in our own voice to write our truth anyway.

### VOICE IN DEVELOPMENT, OVER TIME

Voice reflects where you have been, what you have achieved, and where you are headed. An authentic or "full" voice uses all of our selves, where we are when we write. The more we write, the stronger our voice becomes, analogous to training a speaking or singing voice. We can develop rich tones, favorite nuances and qualities.

And we can expect to see our younger selves in our earlier writing, as Phyllis Hoge Thompson describes here:

> *Phyllis:* It was quite interesting to me to see some of the things that I did a long time ago. I could almost cite the writer that I was imitating. At one point last night when I read "Waiting for Snow" from [my book] The Creation Frame, *I felt very strongly the influence of Rilke there. I probably was quite aware of it when I was writing that poem.*
>
> *I think now that the imitations, or the words that I respond to from other poets, fit more naturally into the poems. You would hardly notice they're there, unless you happen to know the poems they come from.*

Our writing develops and grows; in today's writing, we can find the sprouts of who we are becoming as authors.

## VOICE AS CONVERSATION

Voice may include that function of integration, spinning together voices, again, both in relation to others and within the self. As we write, we are in conversation with our future readers and our various selves.

> Carolivia: *I have many voices. My main writing voice is one that deals with human voices; it weaves them together, rather than a single voice.*

Voice happens when something is struck and something responds. Both author and reader are needed to experience voice: writing voice is heard in the reader, created in the author's writing. The writer first listens to her own writing, asking, *"Is this the most authentic voice I have for this communication?"* (intrapersonal). The reader listens to the author's voice, and responds to her own perception of the authenticity of the writing voice (interpersonal).

## PHYSICAL VOICE AND SCIENCE

Let's ground this question in the physical and consider the current scientific autopsy of voice. All human voice sounds in the English language can be represented by 58 sounds. Today, voice recognition and dictation programs for the computer are available and in common use by lawyers, doctors, researchers, technical writers with carpal-tunnel syndrome, and others. Users can "train" the program to response to their specific voice patterns.

A voiceprint is a visual representation which depicts the version of spoken language unique to each individual person. It is said to be as distinctive for each individual as a fingerprint.

A spectrometer maps the pattern of a person's voice into a voiceprint by tracing the electronic tracks of the vocal chords as they move air through a microphone. From this visual track of vibrations, scientists can tell a person's age, height, and sex from the voiceprint, and can often read the words.

*Voiceprint of a woman in her thirties, saying, "I Gotta Crow."*

Shorter people have a shorter vertical rise to their voiceprint. Women's voiceprints are more rounded than men's. Younger people's vowel asymptotes are more steeply curved.

Security agencies, of course, are extremely interested in speech recognition and voiceprints as we learn to decode them with our technology. Voice recognition scientists agree with Stuart and Graves: [using] voice is like leaving fingerprints.

OUR MAP

From listening to our authors, and mulling over the research, I've come up with three main categories that shape our writing voice.

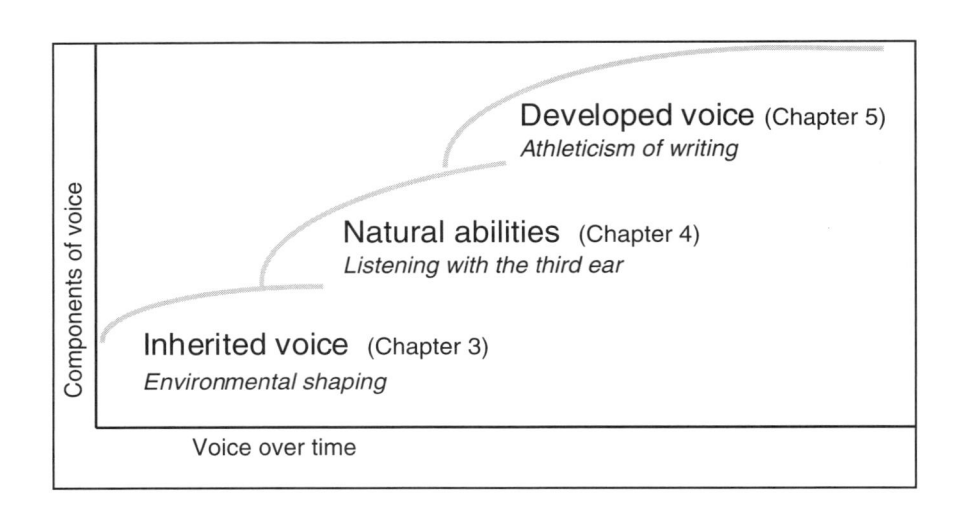

```
Components of voice ↑
                            ╱─────── Developed voice (Chapter 5)
                           ╱          Athleticism of writing
                          ╱
                         ╱──── Natural abilities (Chapter 4)
                        ╱       Listening with the third ear
                       ╱
                      ╱ Inherited voice (Chapter 3)
                        Environmental shaping
                        
                        Voice over time →
```

NOW YOU

» Write your description of your own writing voice or voices. What is important to you about the voice(s) you use in your writing? Keep your description nearby and add notes as we go along.

» Ask several other writers to read something you wrote in voice, and describe your writing voice to you.

# THREE

## *Inherited Voice*

OUR INHERITED VOICE IS HANDED DOWN WITH THE FAMILY FURNITURE. We learn to speak and write in our early environment. The language or languages we hear, and the dialects in which it is spoken select what can be voiced and how it is shaped. Our family's style of communication imprints how comfortable we are with varying distances of intimacy. What is foreground and what is background for us is shaped by our early environment.

### MAPPING ENVIRONMENTS

I imagine several layers of early environment (see the diagram on p. 45)—our family, our schooling or education, the communities we are part of, and our Zeitgeist—the times we live in.

Our authors, in describing their earliest memories of writing, refer to either their family or school. While I did not specifically ask about education, every author spoke of the effect of her education on her writing—positively or negatively. Any of these layers of environment can be seminal. For instance, Yoko Kawashima Watkins's earliest writing memory had the shadow of the war over it, and her life was drastically changed by that Zeitgeist.

### FAMILY ENVIRONMENT

We are located within our position in our own particular family (firstborn, only child, second of five, etc.). Adler and others have written much about the effect of birth order on personality: first-borns become high achievers, while lower birth orders make the best fighter pilots. Second-borns are likely to be more attuned to others' needs than are first-borns. And so on.

Each family has its own particular dynamics. Families can be enmeshed, with close or non-existent boundaries between individuals, sharing secrets or feelings freely and ofttimes passionately expressed. Other families can be disentangled and distant, boundaries clear like closed doors bordering on formal; secrets are assumed, feelings are submerged. Families pass along mantles of expectations to their members, shaping their voice:

> Regina: *I think it was my brother, if anybody, that was supposed to be the writer in the family. . . . It's almost as if we swapped lives. I bet that if my mother had predicted something for each of us, she would have predicted that he would have been a writer and a teacher, and I would have been working, with three kids, and living in Brooklyn. And so it was an interesting thing, somewhere along the way, going to each other, "Huh, I got your script somehow. . . ."*

And here is Montana Miller:

> Montana: *As I grew up, we had this newspaper being published right in our home, and it's been like that since I can remember. My parents started it when I was two years old in our basement, and it's still in our basement.*
>
> *I've always written about everything that's happened to me. It hasn't been a job; it's just my most effective way of communicating.*

For the writer, these family patterns inform how we communicate, our mode and comfort level of intimacy. Do we put our readers metaphorically on our laps, next to us at a table, or across the room? Or do we keep them inside our heads? Are we expressing emotions with fire, or does a lot of the action happen "off screen?" The patterns we learned in our family are those we can most easily begin with in our writing, before we try on other patterns.

The rhythm and sounds of language inform our voice. Growing up hearing a southern drawl affects your voice differently than hearing an Irish brogue. Listening to more than one language from your environment trains your ear. If our family values humor and diversity of input, like Regina Barreca's, then we learn to use humor and diversity.

Our family's language of ideas, what is discussed and what is omitted, trains our vision—what we see and where we put our focus. Barreca's family's ingredients for discussion ranged from *Anna Karenina* to daily details.

> Regina: *My parents were not educated people. Neither of them finished high school. But they were incredibly smart.... I learned very early on that education and intelligence are sometimes coincidental but are not causal. If you're smart ... you can be educated and that's great. Or you can be smart and not educated....*
>
> *Really knowing that at an early age (as opposed to just knowing it theoretically), it wasn't something that came into question. You could talk about incredibly complex ideas in fairly simple language, without simplifying them....*

Yoko Kawashima Watkins's snapshot of dinner conversation tells us about what is valued by her family:

> Yoko: *At suppertime it was just wonderful. Daddy always asked Hideyo [Yoko's brother] about the progress he made. Progress means, he doesn't have to come home with the good grades. Daddy listens to what Hideyo says: "I picked up some strange bug," and we would*

look at the bug under the microscope, his strange colors, things like that. Simple things.

And if there is denial, or non-acknowledgment, this is learned and noted also.

Megan: I know that my parents getting a divorce was a very significant event and I didn't mention it. At the time, I was told not to mention it. My father told us they were getting a divorce, and then we had a birthday party and friends came over to the house for lunch. We were not allowed to tell them. Then my father packed all of his birthday presents and everything in his car and moved to a hotel.

That's how my family dealt with announcing the dissolution of our family as it had been up until that point. And you're surprised I didn't mention it [laughs] in my book!?

### FIRST LANGUAGE

Our first language itself, and how it is spoken, shapes our relationship with our peers. Carolivia Herron shares her early experiences:

Carolivia: I didn't speak black dialect at all. It was always standard English in the home. My mother decided that it was time for me to have more connection with my peers and groups and so forth, and she taught me to speak one of the Paul Lawrence Dunbar dialect poems, which was a joy. The name of the poem is "In the Morning."

I went to school, in the fifth grade, and recited this poem to the class and to the teacher and all.

> *It was my first moment of performance with the first real sense of having done something real and having the adulation of a crowd. The kids in the class thought it was wonderful, and the teacher thought it was so good. I just never had that before.*

Several of our authors are multi-lingual or trained in more than one dialect at an early age: Yoko Kawashima Watkins is Japanese and lived her early life in Korea, then learned English. She has written some books first in Japanese and then translated them into English; others she wrote first in English. Caroline Bird was trained in English, French, Greek, and German.

Regina Barreca and Montana Miller discuss writing in the academic "language" or tongue.

Regina: *It's like learning another language. . . . [W]hat I tell my students is, they need to be able to do that. Especially if they're going to do feminist theory, women's literature. . . . They're going to need to know twice as much. It's like being a foreigner in another country. You have to learn their native tongue. You can't just keep speaking in your own, otherwise you end up in the ghetto. . . .*

*If you want to change the infrastructure, then you have to know how to do everything. . . . We're living in a patriarchal culture. You need to be able to sort of speak in tongues, and then be able to find your own voice.*

Montana: *When I write for academics, I still tend to go for direct clarity. The criticism I get most often from academics is: "This is too journalistic." Because in journalism, clarity, not [being] too wordy, makes it understand-*

*able. Get your point across. That is not what academics want. They want to sound as smart as possible, use the biggest words possible, the most convoluted constructions. . . .*

As a technical writer, I work with engineers, translating into simple terms their abbreviations, technical terms, complexity of knowledge about the machine, and the project code names. I translate to a text that is broken down into simple constructs and pictures, with minimal labels on the drawings, so that it in turn can be easily translated into five languages.

Living with more than one language and/or culture, we can become aware of traditions or cultural assumptions of groups other than those in which we are a direct member.

Caroline Bird told me (off-tape) that when she traveled to Japan in the 1960s, computers were just coming into their golden boom years. She learned that most of the people working on computers in Japan spoke English. She asked why and was told that the Japanese language dealt with the crowding and complexity of its culture partly through the constructive use of ambiguity. Leaving things somewhat indefinite facilitates cooperation more effectively than drawing hard and fast lines. Creating computers required more definiteness and precision than the Japanese language lent itself to. Therefore, at that time, computer scientists used English, valuing its ability to delineate and slice.

### ZEITGEIST

Zeitgeist literally means "spirit of the times." Zeitgeist, like blindspots, also shapes what can be discussed. Some writers have talents to write on the edge of the Zeitgeist. Many of Caroline Bird's books are the advance voice for the Zeitgeist—they push the envelope to talk about what previously has been either not recognized or agreed upon to be ignored, kept in the "what we don't know we don't know" category (see diagram, p. 45).

Even if we are not writing from the voice of the Zeitgeist, our writing reflects and is colored by it. And publishers listen carefully to what the Zeitgeist buys.

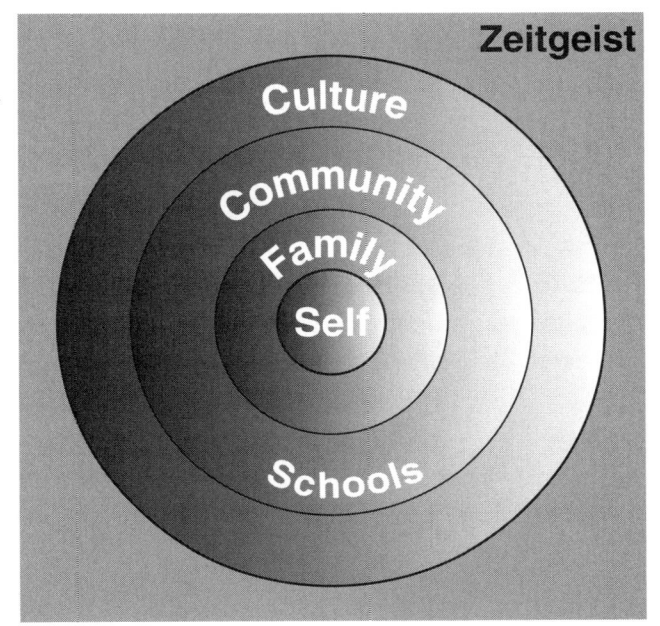

*Environmental layers influencing voice.*

Louise Wisechild, Montana Miller, and Megan LeBoutillier talk about these influences on their writing:

Louise: *I'm really so aware of how astonishingly fortunate I was, when* The Obsidian Mirror *came out. It came out in that tiny little window when you could actually publish work about abuse. But that [window] is closed almost entirely. It is really hard to get that kind of work out now. It has had its little time as a trend.*

Montana: *Well, I would like to write a novel about the Acapulco cliff-diving championships. My agent thinks that it would make a great novel.*

*He asked me to write sample chapters and a plot outline, which I did, and gave to him about a month*

« 45 »

| | |
|---|---|
| | *ago. . . . If he says it's good, if he sells it and I do write the rest of it, that's definitely a different tone than anything I've ever written before: "Lots of paragraphs, action tone, keep the people hooked! Make it a page-turner!" Not so much the poetic writing that I often do about diving.* |
| Megan: | *. . . The Awareness of Possibility. I think it's my best work, but I'm having more trouble getting this one in print. . . . As one agent told me, "Howard Stern's book is on the best-seller list, what can I tell you?" And I said, "I think you've lost the vision of this book. Why don't you send the manuscript back."* |
| | *It's a strange market, you know, it's a strange market. But that's what sells right now. And that's what agents look at: what sells.* |

With 20-20 hindsight, we can see how the Zeitgeist has changed. Discussion of menopause, hormone replacement therapy, and breast cancer is socially acceptable now, no longer reserved only for the privacy of the doctor's office. In the 1950s, none of this was easily discussed, and even less written for general consumption. And *The Vagina Monologues* as a title alone would have been scandalous.

## BLINDSPOTS

Harvard professor of Adult Development Robert Kegan referred to this model (see opposite page) when he was discussing "meaning making." We understand what we know, and we work to understand what we don't know. Yet, there is much that we don't know that we don't know.

These are our blindspots, as writers and people. Each family and culture also has its blindspots, so we inherit those we grow up with, as well. We cannot write from what we don't know, yet our blindspots inform our voice.

Just as we are taught to drive defensively, knowing our cars have blindspots, it is prudent to write with this awareness as well, asking and being ready to react to what is just outside of awareness when it emerges.

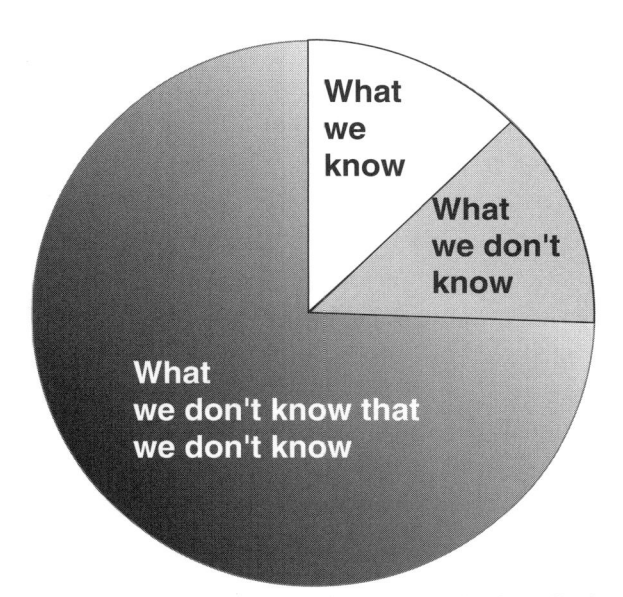

*Diagram attributed to Leland Bradford, National Training Laboratories*

### EARLY MEMORIES

I asked my authors what their earliest memory of writing was, because I wanted to know their earliest roots and to meet them as children, to understand how their creativity, playfulness, and voice were (or were not) nurtured.

> Carolivia: *My earliest memory is [from when I was] about three years old, when I wrote my first poem. My mother read the* Child's Garden of Verses *to me over and over again. I fell in love with the* Child's Garden of Verses, *and I wrote a poem. I didn't know how to write yet, until the following year, so I had to keep it in my head for a year . . . I still think of it as significant, in spite of its simplicity. I thought about it deeply, and made a choice of the words which had a lot of hidden meaning for me.*

## VOICE AND PLAY

Play is an important part of finding voice, because it allows us to try on new selves, like costumes, with sanctuary. We can *pretend* to be, pretend to write *as if*, without committing. And often play allows us to discover our authentic self. I asked our authors what their earliest memories are of writing, and playful scenes were described.

Megan remembers putting books together with ribbon and colored pencils. Louise writes for hours upon hours, quietly grounding with her lock-and-key diary in her lap. Joan is asking questions and wondering about things. Yoko practices her *kanji*, with her canaries nearby. Carolivia is composing a poem silently, taking in all of our voices.

Me? At four, I am making up plays, drawing tickets, and commandeering my cousins as actors and audience; we spring forth from Army blanket curtains tacked in the cellar bulkhead portal, bounding up the stairs, child *deus ex machina* from the theater depths, and *emote*. (I thought this had nothing to do with writing until these interviews.) Regina Barreca said, "Like all kids, I used to make little books. It turns out, that's something a lot of kids do."

Well, I didn't know a lot of kids did this. I remembered, after thinking about what she said, that I have lovingly and carefully saved my very first book that was "bound" with a purple construction-paper cover and "cover art." Written in 1952, it is my first technical manual. I include the cover and first page here (see opposite page).

Through play, by trying on voices, we can also learn our voice by identifying what doesn't ring true.

*Jill:* *Have you ever tried to write in a falsetto?*

*Regina:* *Mm! Yes. . . .*

*Jill:* *And what happens to your writing?*

*Regina:* *It is like watching videos of yourself dancing with tight shoes, or something. It's really very awkward movement.*

Another concept about play is the transitional object. Teddy bears and blankets are toys children typically use as transitional objects, helping them move from one developmental stage into another.

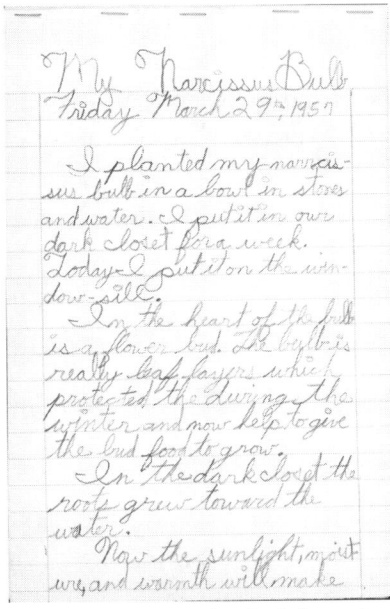

*First book by author.*

Such a comforting object might be reached for in stress or sickness, as a child falls back to earlier developmental stages for comfort. So, too, do writers sometimes have transitional writing voices, falsettos that serve as shields to allow their authentic voice to strengthen and gestate until it can speak strongly.

### VOICE IN ADOLESCENCE

In their collaborative book, *Between Voice and Silence: Women and Girls, Race and Relationship*, authors Jill McLean Taylor, Carol Gilligan, and Amy M. Sullivan conclude a longitudinal study at the Harvard Project on Women's Psychology and Girl's Development. This study interviewed girls: first at age 7, then again at ages 9, 11, 13, and 15. Gilligan, in speaking of this book at the Harvard Faculty Club in February, 1996, said it was absolutely crucial that the book was written collaboratively, because otherwise the researchers might have missed their findings. It was a case of the emperor's new clothes; the researchers could not believe their ears: girls who at age 9 knew what they knew, felt what they felt, and could communicate competently and clearly, by age 13 had dissociated themselves from their own knowing and their voices.

One 13-year-old in the study, when asked what she thought, responded, "Do you want to know what I think, or do you want to know what I really think?" Another 13-year old kept saying, "I don't know," to questions which at 9 she answered clearly. When the interviewer asked, "How is it at 9 you knew this, and at 13 you don't?" the girl answered, "At 9 I was dumb." Why? "Because I was honest."

> Megan: *In the fourth or fifth grade, my English composition teacher wrote in the margin of my paper, "You don't seem to put any of yourself into your work," and I thought, "Hooray! I have managed to successfully erase myself," which was exactly what I intended to do. To this day I don't know whether that was an objection or a compliment to the work.*

Taylor, Gilligan, and Sullivan found, importantly, that the presence of a confiding woman, who could stand outside the culture and affirm the girl's vision through these developmental years, affirming the binds and inequities, was crucial to the survival of the girls' sense of self and of voice.

The silencer has power. The dominant culture defines what is spoken about, what is repressed. The effect on the non-dominant culture (women, or in this case, adolescent girls) is to learn the language of camouflage. She learns to dissociate from her own knowing and her own voice.

When one speaks long enough in a false voice, or with an affected accent, it begins to become a part of identity. Vocal chords can stretch or tighten; patterns set into the face muscles. Changing back to the natural voice requires unlearning.

Girls learn the censorship of the dominant culture. As a minority feminine culture, we are learning to mask our voices. We learn to disguise those voiceprint gender differences, to dissociate from them, to speak and write, like the Canadian freelancer (see p. 31), with the voice of the "client," the one in power.

Taylor, Gilligan, and Sullivan's study highlights the importance of the presence of a woman in relationship to the girl, willing to stand outside the dictates of the immediate culture and confirm the perception distortion being imposed on the girl. The existence of this older woman confidante is significant to the recovery of self and voice for the emerging adolescent-woman.

For some of our authors presented here, writing itself was such a confidante. It kept their voices alive.

### MATRIARCHAL LINEAGE

I have co-led women's workshops in which we begin each meeting in a circle. Each woman in turn speaks her name—but not only her name, but that of her daughter or daughters (if she has them), and her mother, her grandmother, and as far back as she can go.

Typically, at the first meeting, most women can remember their grandmother's name, maybe their great-grandmother's. But some women's names, like our voices, have gotten lost or misplaced. By the second meeting, most everyone has discovered more family names. And it is very moving to hear the names repeated around the room, and listen to the older names coming back.

My introduction goes like this:

> *I am Jill, mother of Anne who has taught me loving patience, daughter of Florence who gave me love of teaching, grand-daughter of Della who gave me laughter and puns, great-granddaughter of Amanda and great-great-granddaughter of Della.*

In these family photos, my mother, my daughter, and I are all pictured in our twenties. You can see some of the imprint of our Zeitgeist—the styles of the early 1940s, late 1960s, and 1990s, and what was considered feminine. The grandmothers are pictured at older ages, but the styles of their time are still visible.

Culturally, the grandmothers and my mother are 100% Pennsylvania Dutch Mennonite and Lutherans. I'm half Pennsylvania Dutch and half Irish, and my daughter Anne adds more Yankee. All, with the exception of Anne, were born and raised within a 10-mile area of Bucks County, Pennsylvania (halfway between Philadelphia and Allentown).

We lived in the boroughs of Blooming Glen, Silverdale, Perkasie, and Sellersville—initially quiet farm towns with rolling hills, now morphed into busier bigger communities with many commuters. Small towns are closed systems; if I went to the bank and the drug store after school, by dinner my parents knew where I'd been without my telling them. Everyone knows your name, if the town is small enough—you are not invisible.

Folks watched out for each other. Those who broke the rules were remembered, so mostly folks followed them.

[Left to right] My great-great-grandmother Della Long (b. ~1840); great-grandmother Amanda Hunsberger Long (b. 1861); grandmother Della Mae Long (b. 1881).

With roots in one place through that many generations, extended family abounded. Family picnics were large, pot-luck events. In addition to many traditional relatives of aunts, uncles, and cousins, I have second cousins once removed, third cousins on my mother's side (you learned to conjugate the family tree pretty early on).

*My mother Florence Moyer Hackett (b. 1919); me (b. 1947); and my daughter Anne Long Fifield (b. 1970), all pictured in their twenties.*

And then there are all of the imaginary aunts and uncles—close family friends over decades. My parents played bridge with the same four tables of people for over 50 years, and they are all my "aunts" and "uncles," too.

In the 1950s, the whole community was like this—filled with families that had lived there for several generations. My generation was the first to move away in large numbers after school—influences of the 1960s—to start their families elsewhere.

Making a living was a family business for great-grandmother Amanda. Her husband made roll-top carriages, and she raised children, horses, and crops.

My grandmother Della was an equestrian, a musician, and made the most marvelous applesauce and silly jokes. Widowed in her early forties with four small children, she broadened her piano teaching to support her family.

My mother and her two sisters were career women, at a time when society placed value on women staying home. Mother taught public kindergarten for 15 years, founded and ran a private nursery school for 15 years, and then managed an antique shop for another 15 years. I come from a long line of working women.

All of the grandmothers could speak Pennsylvania Dutch to some degree, and I learned to do a fairly decent accent by listening to my mother and her sisters tease each other with it. I did not learn the language, though I heard it from time to time (my grandmother mostly grumbled in Pennsylvania Dutch).

So my inherited voice was formed by the strong moral codes of a small town—"Be very conscious how your communication affects others." I was taught to speak, however, by independent self-employed women who were used to trusting their own decisions.

And the music and nuances of language have long held a special fascination for me. I think the Irish side may help explain my love of language for its own sake!

## NOW YOU

- » Trace your own voice lineage. It may be matriarchal, patriarchal, or a combination.

- » What blindspots have you inherited? What particularly keen sight is yours?

- » What traditions color your voice?

- » Talk with family or close friends, and consider their impact on your voice. With whom can you speak unedited? With whom is your voice muffled?

- » Draw a voice tree, tracing the roots of your voice.

- » What teachers have been instrumental to you? Describe their voice.

## FOUR

## *Natural Abilities*

Listening is input for writers. It is how we gather our raw material. Not just listening with our physical ears, but listening to writers when we read, listening to media when we are bombarded by it, listening to colleagues and friends, listening to our own gut. It means listening with all our intelligences, all our ways of knowing, with our "third ear."* And, to find our authentic voice, it especially means listening to our core.

> *The psychologist has to learn how one mind speaks to another beyond words and in silence. He must learn to listen "with the third ear."* [Reik, p. 144]

This is equally true for writers. Writing with voice speaks clearly to another mind "beyond words and in silence."

Author and actor Anna Deveare Smith performs listening. She makes it visible. In her *1992: Twilight Los Angeles*, she interviewed people within a few degrees of the Rodney King trial: Rodney's aunt, a truckdriver witness, lawyers, as well as leaders of affected communities. Then she took verbatim excerpts from these interviews, studied the voice and mannerisms of the speaker, and "performed" the interviews for us. Remember the picture in our science books from elementary school that showed the scientist's conception of how a fly sees out of

---

* Theodor Reik's *Listening with the Third Ear* (1948) takes this phrase from Nietzsche, *Beyond Good and Evil, Part VIII*, p. 246.

each of its multiple ocular cells? I felt like an audial cell in the collective audience of Smith's ears. I saw, heard, experienced a piece of how she listens. She shows how we don't listen carefully enough to what we say.

A good piece of writing will likewise invite us into the author's inner mind, listening to her voice in her writing, experiencing through her.

When we are writing, we often become keenly aware of information, serendipities that relate to what we are writing about. Much like when you are shopping for a new home, you'll go to a friend's house and suddenly notice the layout of the kitchen, or the baseboards or cornices. Just so, our attention gets focused on what our mind is "hunting."

We can also train ourselves to listen for details that will be helpful in future writing, to bag material as we go along in everyday life, noticing its fullness and richness.

I had the privilege of meeting young-adult author Robert Cormier (*I Am the Cheese*, *The Chocolate War*). Robert was talking away, telling me how he writes, and he said:

> *If it's an action scene I'll try to get that forward movement and that thrust. Once I have that locked in, then I go back and layer in the setting, just the action between two people sitting there talking. Like me talking with my hands a lot and you not. I might write that in.*

Here, he gesticulated a lot, and then held his arms quietly to his body. I became instantly aware that Robert was acutely listening, kinetically, to me, even while he was engaged in speaking. He was taking in details of my watching, recording. I was indeed keeping myself very still, trying to listen as completely as I could. Meanwhile, he was gathering material.

I have heard that for writers, there are no bad experiences, just more raw material.

How we listen is partially shaped by our inherited voice, how our ear was trained. It is also partially shaped by our own factory modeling. Like cars, each of us is shipped out with special features right from the factory, our own unique packaging that sets us apart as individuals even within our families. One might be especially talented at empathy, while another of us is musical, able to carry a tune even before we could speak.

## SEVEN INTELLIGENCES

Harvard educator and researcher Howard Gardner proposes that human beings have several intelligences. In his book, *Frames of Mind: The Theory of Multiple Intelligences*, Gardner describes seven intelligences (allowing that there are probably more). They are:

linguistic • logical-mathematical

interpersonal • intrapersonal • spatial

musical • kinesthetic

Let's look at some of the ways our authors use these "intelligences" as modes of listening and writing.

## LINGUISTIC INTELLIGENCE

A love of words and language can be heard in many of our interviews. Writers often have a fondness for words, collecting them, ever aware of the shades of meaning. Yoko calls it a "special play" with words. Carolivia admits she "loves all the words, all the adjectives." Joan recalls searching for just the right word in an elementary school essay.

I was relieved to find this love of words in our authors. I can lose myself in any bookstore just browsing. Sometimes I sit with a thesaurus and a dictionary and play, opening one at random and reading, finding a word I like the sound of and excavating its meanings. I like that words have at least two shades: what it means void of political dressings (denotation), and what it has come to mean in a particular culture (connotation). The most beautiful sounding word I've encountered so far is *ferrocarril,* Spanish for "train."

Linguistic intelligence is similar to musical. But linguistic intelligence deals with fine-tuning our sensitivity to words, alone and in strings of meaning, in narrative, while musical intelligence is concerned with fine-tuning sound along with meaning.

The poet searches for both. Our poet, Phyllis Hoge Thompson, has rich linguistics intelligence, as can be seen in this autobiographical piece published in a poetry anthology*:

Phyllis: *I have cared about words for as long as I can remember. My mother fostered and fortified that love.*

*My mother read poems to me before I could read them to myself, and she put the right books into my hands while I was still very young. . . . by the time I was twelve, I had played with every metrical convention and rhymed-stanza form described by whoever wrote the narrow red book I trusted. . . .*

*I love figuring out which words sound truest and best, I love how they fit into a line or a sentence or a phrase.*

*I love their weight, I love all they assemble of thought or feeling. What they remind me of apart from what I have chosen to say.*

*I love how they're spelled and where they came from.*

*I love working out in lines their music, which is for me very securely based in the old-fashioned metrics I learned before I grew up.*

*I love fitting everything together and I love finding out what the poem says when at last it feels right.*

---

* From the prize-winning book, *What the Land Gave* (Vol. XXII of the Quarterly Review of Literature Poetry Book Series).

Phyllis starts with words at the top of her page, like a painter mixing her paints, before she starts a poem:

*"... a rainbow of words across the top of the page, just—I have no idea what their relationship is, just words that I feel like bringing forward at that moment, and they just kind of scatter across the top of the page and down the side margin."*

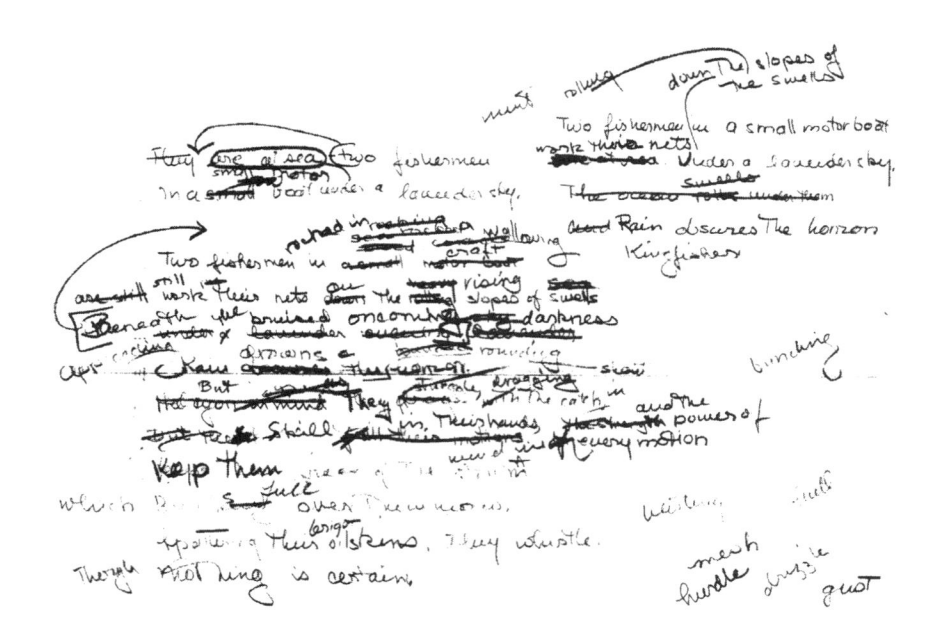

And here, Phyllis's finished poem*:

FRIENDS

                          for Janet Fredericks

Beneath a muscular dusk
And a storm coming on fast,
Two fishermen, rocked in a bucking craft,
Still work their nets on the plunging slopes of the sea swells.
They shout to each other
As they struggle dragging the catch in,
All steel and dull silver.
Rain drowns the rounding horizon,
And now the bruised clouds crack open
In driving gusts, spattering their oilskins.
The men keep an eye on the weather but go on hauling,
Hunched over the ropes or standing braced,
Balanced in the baffling wind.
Their trust rests in the skill of their hands
And the power of their arms spread wide, or strained, pulling.

Wet-faced, they grin.
This is not the first time they've tackled the Atlantic
Late, under a nightfall sky green as tornado.
And it's not the last.
Their trust in each other is steadfast
And commonplace.
They're out there alive at work in the driving rain
On the cold salt water.

                          —Phyllis Hoge Thompson

---

*Copyright Phyllis Hoge Thompson. Reprinted with permission.

Linguistic intelligence can start very young, as it did with Phyllis, and with Joan Hiatt Harlow:

> Joan: *I was probably only six or seven. I was searching for a word and I used a thesaurus to find a word with the proper beat, the proper rhythm, so that it would work in that poem.... I really loved the power of words. I really, really felt a sense of fulfillment in being able to share this.*

As we noted earlier, growing up with more than one language or dialect "tunes" the linguistic ear for writing. It can provide sensitivity to language—and extra challenges. Listen to Carolivia Herron and Yoko Kawashima Watkins:

> Carolivia: *The tension between the black dialect and the Standard English became a very intriguing connection for me, which comes out in my writing. If you saw my book* Asenath *that* Nappy Hair *is taken from, this is the only part in African-American dialect, in the whole book. It is a book of Standard English, but this crucial central moment* has *to go into the African-American speech patterns.*

> Yoko: *It is very difficult for me, because I am an English-as-a-second-language person. I often use Japanese expressions. Still, I can't translate it directly into charming English. So what do I do? I frustrate. But I do the best of it. I think and walk a little bit, I depend on Japanese-to-English and English-to-Japanese dictionaries.*
>
> *Then if I could not find any words, I just vacuum the whole house. Maybe you can jog, but in my case,*

*I clean the whole house, vacuum very frantically, and then I calm myself down.*

*And I often do the Tea Ceremony, knowing the way of the Tea.*

### LOGICAL-MATHEMATICAL INTELLIGENCE

Logical-mathematical intelligence helps us with structure—those steel girders I mentioned in the Preface. It helps us with building the blueprint of our pieces, and seeing the x-ray of the structure. Caroline Bird's research, for instance, is well-ordered and thorough, establishing a good logical path throughout—an essential element for a writer like her who is writing social commentary, breaking new ground in advocacy for women's issues.

Also, we can use this intelligence when a piece doesn't "hang together," when some bridge needs to be built, to allow the creative sides and the organizing sides to work well together.

Jill: *My main writing voice is this logical, mathematical rational mechanical voice, which the technical writing has trained.*

*Allowing any other range of voice now has been difficult until I found a way to use that technical voice in service of the others.*

*And so I have given that persona the task of organization and craft, dealing with the authoring software and technology.*

### INTERPERSONAL INTELLIGENCE

This combines your instincts and the ability to connect to your audience—the relational aspect we discussed in the chapter *Describing Voice*.

When I first met her, I asked Phyllis why she wrote. "For the audience," she said. Joan writes because: "I believe in the story. Characters are so real to me that it's almost as if they must live." This intelligence is the "connecting" part of "writing to connect." Stephen King in his book *On Writing* talks about writing as a telepathic communication that is delivered in a time warp; he creates pictures he wants his readers to see. They will not receive them until months or years after he has written them. But he holds his audience present in his mind when he writes.

Regina Barreca's books are an ongoing conversation with her readers:

> *Regina:* It is like a running conversation. I sit down at the computer and I have a sense of who my readers are ... I got comfortable, talking to women my age.
> "My age" is now anybody who is too old for work-study and too young for Medicare: 18 to 60.
>
> In our most intimate lives, we have incredibly similar experiences. We get our buttons pushed because the culture has planted those buttons, so they know how to push them.

## INTRAPERSONAL INTELLIGENCE

This is listening to your own voice centers; our inner dialogue is deciphered with this intelligence.

Two images represent the intrapersonal for me. One is the folk art of a bird, its head bent in a loop with its beak upon its own breast. The other is a picture I saw of a pregnant woman with a stethoscope, listening to the life in her womb. Intrapersonal is what Phyllis Hoge Thompson terms "interior listening." Let's listen to Carolivia Herron and Megan LeBoutillier:

> *Carolivia:* My main writing voice is one that deals with human voices: it weaves them together, rather than a single

*voice. I'm recovering from multiple-personality disorder, so this is not just something I'm making up as a technique, but as a way my mind has worked for much of my life, and if you look at many of my writings, you'll find that there is a single voice. . . . a strong major personality that pulls the other ones together. The others are in conversation with each other, and the major voice . . . looks over, hears them, and then speaks them out. . . .*

Megan: *. . . an autobiographic journal-writing segment in which I separated out and identified multiple internal personalities that I named and made very specific and real in my life. I orchestrated dialogue between them, I used them. And figured out just what all the hum had been in my mind for years.*

*Then . . . I used those characters to describe a process to get back in touch with my creative process. That was the book about families and alcoholism. And I was in the book this time, because I belonged in the book, from the very first, and so the whole thing . . . went full circle.*

Without intrapersonal listening, we might erase ourselves from our writing.

### MUSICAL INTELLIGENCE

Musical intelligence in writing orchestrates cadence, alliteration, onomatopoeia, and harmony, playing with the sound of words. It informs sentence structure and images, and the inner harmony of thoughts and structures. This quality is what is typically called "having a good ear." Read your writing into a tape recorder and listen to it, or read it aloud to a friend. Poet Donald Hall dictates most of his poetry first, then reads it on paper. When we read writing aloud and hear with the physical ear, we often find new understandings, or hear miscommunications that the work carries because this technique invokes the "signwave" auditorily, the discernable pattern underneath the words that carries voice.

Phyllis describes her writing voice as musical. As a child, she won a contest writing about music, though she knew very little about the subject. Her childhood essay was musical itself, echoing the concert in her words, rather than theory and critique of the concert.

> Phyllis: *What I did really was not an exercise in music appreciation, although I know that the judges thought it was. Because what I wrote was musical.*
>
> *It was a scrapbook about the five concerts, and it contained a poem and I probably drew a picture, but it had nothing to do with the music. [Laughs]*

And we use musical intelligence to listen to pacing:

> Joan: *If you get to a sluggish point, you've lost the audience. You want to keep a pace. It's similar to a ballgame or a dance.*

### SPATIAL INTELLIGENCE

The ability to visualize or recall detail is helpful for creating writing that can transmit three-dimensional images to the reader. Some writers layer in these spatial/visual details after plot and structure, while others of us may begin with the images. Carolivia Herron's writing (and mine) often starts with inner pictures, which she then translates into words.

> Carolivia: *I am so abstract, mythical and poetic in my writing ... I almost need a plot, or a hint of a plot,*

> *or something to pull it into the world people see.... That's the reason why I talk about the visions I can see. To me, it is like this table, but since other people can't see it, it is hard to convey what I've imagined. With the power of the computer, I can convey it, along with the words.*

Jill: *I think in pictures ... I "see" or sense an image on an inner screen.... and then put words to them.*

## KINESTHETIC INTELLIGENCE

This refers to feeling your writing in your gut, or in your head. We write from different voice centers, using different parts of our body for different voices and purposes. Paying attention to your full-bodied experience as you're writing is useful to help keep focused and stay in the flow.

It can also be used to develop stories and characters. Rachel Vail walks around in her characters, exploring their physicality before she commits them to paper:

Rachel: *I try to find who my character is physically.... I try to figure out where the character holds her weight, how the character sits, where she clenches when she's tense, what she does with her fingers when she's nervous, how she stands when she feels confident, and how she stands when she's feeling awkward. I try to get inside the physicality of my character.*

## COMMUNITY INTELLIGENCE

Most of our women authors talk about their communities. They are sensitive to how their writing informs, creates, furthers the communities they contribute to and live in. This is different from looking at the more personal aspects of self or a small group. And this "attending to community" fits with current research on women's attention to relationships. Let's listen to Carolivia Herron, Louise Wisechild, and Yoko Kawashima Watkins:

*Carolivia:* *I think you would see the interest in creating an oral story for my group, my group being many particular groups: I am African-American, I am Jewish . . . and I am of course a woman. I am a U.S. American. And all those sorts of things come together in my wanting to tell the story about epic. . . .*

*I think the 21st century needs that epic—we need to open up the new century with the concept that it is possible not to lose artistic value even when you have many voices.*

*Louise:* *I began to realize that what I had hoped—which is that [my book] would help people—was happening. I was so lucky in that a lot of people who read my book wrote to me. I felt connected with the outer world and other survivors of childhood abuse for the first time. That experience for me was also really, really powerful.*

*Yoko:* *I was not going to be a writer. I was going to be a mother, which is very important, to send balance to kids, to well-balance the kids to the society. Not everyone can be a mother, you know. I was going to be a super mother like my own mother. But somehow I kind of fell into this occupation, and it is good. I go around to schools and tell the children, "Wake up and be humble."*

*Illustration by Betty LaDuke.*

### WRITER AS LEADER

Howard Gardner's book *Leading Minds: An Anatomy of Leadership* defines a leader as someone who listens to her community and can give voice to its story in such a way that others are inspired by her voice and want to follow. A voiceful writer, by this definition, is leader of her readership.

*A leader is an individual who creates a story that significantly affects the thoughts, behaviors, and feelings of a significant number of persons who then become followers. Since followers invariably know many stories, a leader can only be effective if his or her story is powerful and if it can compete successfully for influence with already prevalent stories. The most powerful stories turn out to be about identity: stories that help individuals discover who they are, where they are coming from, where they are headed. A crucial element in the effectiveness of a story hinges on whether the leader's own actions and way of life embody and reinforce the themes of this story.*\*

Gardner further defines direct and indirect leaders:

*Some . . . leaders provide indirect leadership through the powerful symbolic products that they create. We think of Jean-Jacques Rousseau, John Henry (Cardinal) Newman, and John Dewey in this vein. Other leaders provide direct leadership through the stories that they communicate to students, faculty, and other constituents.*\*

This reminds me of the theory that we talked about in Chapter One: The most honorable profession is teacher, so that you may have students (direct leadership). Barring this, if you write a book, you may have students, but at a distance (indirect leadership). Yoko Kawashima Watkins' mothering of her family was direct leadership, and writing her books, for her, is helping to "balance the children to the culture," or indirect leadership.

Carolivia Heron refers to this concept also when she discusses praise song. The praise singer, with little or no direct leadership, influences listeners through indirect leadership:

Carolivia: The context of the praise singer, in the African communities—what do you actually do to keep the kings and the nobles in line? If people are being praised, and to make sure [they stay in line], "You

---

\* From Howard Gardner's *Leading Minds: An Anatomy of Leadership*. New York: Basic Books, 1995.

*wouldn't do such-and-such, would you? Because you are so wonderful! Therefore you would not hurt the this-one and the that-one and the other." It is a way of controlling when there isn't any real power to control but there is verbal power and cultural power to help make the people who are high and praiseworthy be praiseworthy, be heroic, and of course that's one of the things I'm after.*

### LISTENING TO OURSELVES

How we hear our own voice is usually quite different from how others hear us.

Our physical voice sounds different to us on a tape recorder, because we are hearing our external voice, listening the same way we listen to others. When we hear our own physical voice as we are using it, we have all the internal sonic feedback and vibrations from our bones and cavities, which changes the sound. We are receiving the sound waves inside out.

Similarly, our writing voice sounds different to us. We may often take for granted our own natural intelligences, since they come easily to us. They are second nature to us, and observations and information gained from them seem almost obvious to us. It is easy to think they are obvious to all others. Not so, of course.

Many of our authors speak about having to learn to value their inner dialogue, what comes naturally for them in writing. By honoring our process and listening to what our writing says easily, we can begin to know our own writing voice.

> Megan: *When I started writing, [fiction] was not what started to come out. And I just tried and tried and tried and tried to make that come out. It was a long time before I got out of my way and realized* this *flows [gestures to the right], and* this *doesn't [gestures to the left].*

*And I didn't know what* this *[gestures to the right], what I did, was called....*

*So I finally just decided, "Well, let's listen to what it is that you have to say, what just comes out of you easily. Let's not worry about the name of the genre, and if it's justified. Let's just see what comes out."*

*I hadn't known what to call it until ... I discovered creative nonfiction. And then it was like, "Oh yes, yes, yes, yes, that's a name that fits for me."*

Use these intelligences as a starting point to pinpoint your voice's natural talents.

### NOW YOU

» Identify your primary and secondary intelligences.

» Which intelligence do you use with each of your genres? Is your dominant intelligence the same across genres, or does it change?

» Is there an intelligence you have that you could use more fully in your writing? How do you use it now? How could you use it? What do you need to take advantage of that talent?

» With a fellow writer, discuss this chapter. Limiting yourself to only 3 minutes, each talk about what struck you the most. Then reflect back to each other what intelligences you heard the other person use, and how. Respond with how these actually do (or could) show up in your writing.

# FIVE

## Developed Voice

Developed voice is about what we do with what we've got, building on what we were given (inherited voice). It is product of our workouts with our writing. And it is also about others' response to our natural intelligences and inherited voice—and how we react to that.

We have varying degrees of comfort in expressing ourselves. This partly has to do with our education—formal or informal. How much information do we have available to us, how easily can we find a word? Have we been listened to, encouraged—or ignored and made invisible? And what did we do with those experiences? Did we redouble our intentions to communicate, or fold?

Reluctance to speak up can also carry over to reluctance to write with voice. And then there is motivation. As Joan Hiatt Harlow said, "Talent is one thing, and the drive to express it, another."

### THE WOUNDED WRITER

Megan LeBoutillier used the term "creative wound."

There is an archtype of the wounded healer. The theory is that one needs to go through a healing crisis oneself, facing death or near death, before one can come into the fullness of her healing power. Only though the alchemy of this kind of transformation, then, can one understand and minister to others in healing.

Wounding may not be necessary to attain depth of voice. But if one has been through a crisis—creative or personal, that crisis can be used in service of strengthening voice. And clarifying voice.

Noted American anthropologist Margaret Mead talks about this in her book *Blackberry Winter*—the frost bringing out the sweetness of the fruit. There is something about hard times that brings a choice: either resiliency, and we grow and strengthen from it, or we give up and fold. Collapse can be a protective choice, when one needs time to heal and regain resources before resiliency can return.

And our voices get clarified by the scarring.

> *Megan:* *I think of the time when my mother found the stories and laid them on my bed as a creative wound, that that effectively silenced my public voice.*
>
> *. . . being a writer is a lifelong dream, and somewhere along the line I realized that I had released the dream or been separated from it or something. At some point it became very important that I get back in touch with that dream. And I appreciate now being on the other side of the struggle, that I really had to work very hard for something.*

Yoko Kawashima Watkins and Joan Hiatt Harlow both had the experience of wounding by elementary teachers when the teacher jeered their young stories—both about birds. For each of them, it brought up a determination to stand by her truth.

At age 7, Yoko wrote her first story born out of challenge to her truth. When she was young, Yoko's physical voice was weak and whispery, and she learned to speak more audibly by talking to her birds. The class bully and then the teacher did not believe that the bird helped her get her voice, and called her a liar. Yoko endured this round, and then another blow sent her from the school—and to writing her first published story. She tells this story in her interview.

And Joan's bird story:

> *Joan:* *I wrote a story in second or third grade about a wounded bird that I took care of until it could fly.*

*The teacher called me to her desk and told me, "This couldn't happen. The bird could never fly again."*
*I tried to explain that it was a "make-believe" story but I ended up feeling as if I had told a terrible lie.*
*I guess she didn't know about "that willing suspension of disbelief which constitutes poetic faith."*

*Later when I gave her a poem I had worked on at home, she didn't believe I had written it. But other teachers did recognize my writing abilities and were really encouraging, later.*

### HIATUS FROM WRITING

Half of our women authors talked about a hiatus from writing, some time when they stopped writing completely. Several used the term "going underground," and I could not help but think of the Persephone-Demeter mother-daughter myth. And again, *Blackberry Winter*, an autumn-wintering cycle in the unconscious. When the writing re-emerged, it was often with renewed vigor.

Sometimes the hiatus was not chosen but caused, imposed from without rather than from within. Joan Hiatt Harlow experienced what American psychologist Harry Stack Sullivan calls "disasters in timing" when, as her writing career was lifting off, her family got sandbagged with challenges and she, as caretaker, "lost myself for a few years."*

### "SEPARATION AND INDIVIDUATION" OF VOICE

My son Matthew, when his voice was changing, would answer the telephone in a deep voice. I knew if it was a girl phoning, because if it was, Matt would keep talking this funny new way, and if it wasn't, his voice

---

* TILLIE OLSEN'S ELOQUENT BOOK *Silences* DISCUSSES THIS IN MORE DEPTH. SEE ALSO OUR DISCUSSION OF "A MATTER OF TIME" ON P. 80.

would rise up and crack. As his voice changed, he tried on different ways of talking.

So also, when we write, we may try on voices. To find our own voice, we need to distinguish our own voice from those we have borrowed or have had imposed on us. First, we separate our voice from our parents. Then, as we learn to write, we separate out the voices of the authors we have studied and admired.

Montana Miller learned to write from her mother, Kathleen Cushman. They both told me Montana's current writing task is to separate their voices.

Montana: *And a lot of times the result is that I'm not really sure whose work it is. When we co-authored a book, that was okay, because that's the goal ... But, when it's important—and sometimes it is very important—for me to write something that is mine, because she is available to me, and willing, and I enjoy working with her so much, and I know that it's helpful to the quality of my writing, then I have to be careful about defending what is my work against ...*

*It feels strange to say, because I'm not talking about defending my writing—it's like, I'm opening my arms to the thing I should be defending against. It doesn't feel like an attack. But in some ways, I know it's destructive to my own growth as a writer and as a person. And I have to force myself to separate from my mother in a lot of ways.*

Phyllis Hoge Thompson can see, with 20-20 hindsight, some of the voices influencing her early poetry. Here is her answer to "how has your writing voice changed over time?"

Phyllis: *I became more confident of my ability to say what I wanted, and not worry about whether I was going to have the ability to say it. I began feeling as though I could say it, whatever I wanted to say I would find the right words.*

*My poems became less imitative—far more my own. It just happened.*

## THE ATHLETICISM OF WRITING

We have a myth that the Muse visits, like the tooth fairy, giving inspiration. This can of course happen, but in its own unique, un-forcible timing. Until then, and to woo the Muse, we need to sweat.

Rachel Vail touched on this myth first in my interviews, when she talked about the athleticism of writing:

Rachel: *What really turned the corner for me, in being able to write, was this playwriting professor, who said, "Of course your first 20 ideas are going to be ridiculous—you've heard them already! . . . Vomit those out, get past those first 20 or 40 or 50 things, just cross those out. Delete them, throw them in the garbage . . . it's going to be the 51st, that might be the beginning of something worth working on."*

*That gave me the permission to be trite. . . . so that first sentence doesn't have to be brilliant, because of course it's not going to be.*

*You just need to get it out. And writing became less exalted. And more athletic. . . .*

*You are getting there, and you stretch and you try, and you keep trying, and you get sweaty and dirty, and you just keep going. It is not going to come out poetry, literally, on your first effort. . . . You just keep going and going.*

*It gave me permission not to have to be Mozart. I figured out that I had to keep making stuff up until it becomes true. It wasn't going to be true the first time I sat down.*

Carolivia Herron works out in silence:

*Carolivia:* *Everything I publish is read aloud many, many, many times. So many times, it is embarrassing to say. I start at the beginning of a paragraph, and I read one sentence, and I wait. I look up and I wait to see what word comes next in my head.*

*And if the word that comes next in my head is not the one that I have written, then I work it over again, until the silence fills automatically with the next word. And then I do that and then I read two sentences—*

*I will do that over and over again until I get one paragraph. And then I do the next paragraph, and then I read two paragraphs, and then on and on like that, in any one paragraph.*

*And I walk. I like to have places where I can walk around in a circle. The beach is good for it. And it takes hours and hours.*

*That's the kind of silence and the actual process of writing.*

Caroline Bird adds another facet when she discusses the myth that creative work somehow exists somewhere already: like Michelangelo, we just need to find it in the marble and let it express itself. For her, the truth is that she is creating something new that was not there before—a bit sweatier task than "allowing."

## DISCIPLINE

This is that aphorism: "It doesn't matter how good you are, it's how bad you want it."

Joan Hiatt Harlow taught elementary children a course she designed called "The writing game." I asked her if she could identify potential writers in young children:

> Joan: *The most creative people are not the most productive because they may not have that drive to produce. They are not builders. Talent is one thing and the drive to express it is another.*
>
> *Someone may have talent and great ideas, but give up or not work on it. Someone else may not have as much talent, but work at it more and perfect it.*
>
> *The drive allows one to succeed.*

Dorothea Brande advises writing every day, even just 300 words. In her words from her 1934 book, *Becoming a Writer*, this commitment is a "debt of honor." Like brushing your teeth, it must become non-negotiable, so that eventually you no longer doubt if you can write a page a day, you just do it. And the words and pages mount up.

This is the feel-the-burn part. Caroline Bird said to me, "Suppose you have 27 hours in a day. God has given everyone else 24, but you have 27 for now. What will you do with those extra three hours? What do you really want to do?"

I answered, "I'd take a walk in the woods every morning with my dogs, and then I'd write. I'd write everything in my head, and then I'd go out and research, fill it up some more, and write some more."

She replied, "You're not going to get those extra three hours a day. You have to make them."

## A MATTER OF TIME

There is a myth that one needs to make huge caverns of quiet time to write. The reality is that most writers begin in the margins of their unquiet life, and move to full-time writing as occupation only after many years. Some of my authors were hard to reach: they were on speaking tours, lecturing, doing book signings, radio shows. This "other work" supported the time for "real" writing.

Writing in the margins becomes especially complicated for women with work, relationship, and children. The myth of needing time to write full-time may be confused with the need for some combination of solitude, silence, and stillness in order to write. Jacquelyn Mitchard writes about the Ragdale Foundation's writer-artist colony, a place *"for people who don't have the time or money in their lives to finish creative projects—which is, I guess, most people."*\* She notes that more really successful novelists are men, while most Ragdale residents are women.

> *It would be easy to say that imbalance exists because women tend to have less time (and the inclination to give less time) to their creative work. It's easy to say that because it's true. . . . my four times as a Ragdale fellow—a total of two months—have constituted the only real period of solitude and self-indulgence in my adult life.*
>
> *These periods have been the only time I've had food prepared for me, other than when I was recovering from surgery or caring for a newborn. . . . It's been the only time I've had custody of my own purpose. . . .*
>
> *The gift is time. It's like the feeling of having mobility restored to an injured limb. First strange, almost painful, then hourly, more powerful and restorative.*

---

\* JACQUELYN MITCHARD, FROM HER COLUMN, *The Rest of Us*, "FOR WOMEN WRITERS, QUIET TIME IS GOLDEN," *The Sun*, CHICAGO (SUNDAY, APRIL 10, 1997).

"Custody of my own purpose." As a single mother for 19 years, I felt I had shared custody of my own purpose. Phyllis Hoge Thompson picks up these themes and elaborates:

Phyllis: *When I was having babies I just didn't have time to write. So as soon as I stopped having babies and finished my Ph.D., I started.*

*I think time has been a critical matter ... although I've done some writing in the past three years, whenever I've been to Yaddo or some other artist's colony, I've been able to pour myself into the work.*

*Now I think I can do it at home, because I can see some time ahead of me. . . .*

*I think that something that comes up is the question of children, doesn't it? For all but male writers—maybe them also? I'm very grateful that I had children, and grateful that I have grandchildren.*

*I think that having children turns women outside of themselves ... this is a crazy generalization—that mothers have to become less self-centered as they grow older, and I think that when you become less self-centered you can deal with problems that occur to people other than yourself. You can deal with them honestly.*

*... it follows from the fact that initially your self is taken away from you. You have an experience in which you can't devote yourself to yourself. So that you're open to more. Which forces you to look away from yourself toward others. When you come back, to having time, to explore who it is you are ...*

Jill: *You've popped your kernel. You can never go back into that little shell.*

*Phyllis:   Right. You're much more open, I think. And you can write with interest and attention to things outside of yourself, it seems to me.*

## VOICE AS DEFENSE

In a self-defense class, our instructor Peg taught that the voice is always the first line of defense. "Speak up. If you are being attacked, yell. It helps retard shock and shallow breathing. If you yell, your lungs fill up and you are more grounded and present than if you move into a flight response." Peg instructs our class of 18 women to stomp our feet and yell "No!" then scream "911" all together.

We do this, loudly. A good deal of sound comes out. Then we laugh, a bit uncomfortable from our uncharacteristic shout. But one young woman is in tears. Peg, our instructor, asks her, "What's going on?" The twenty-something woman says, "I've never yelled 'NO!' before, and it scared me. And it felt so *good*."

Peg gives each of us a post-a-note and tells us to write our name on it, then put it on the floor. One by one, we each do this exercise. "Keep one foot on your name. It is you that you are protecting. Now draw a circle in the air all around you; that is your boundary." The "mugging" instructor approaches and taunts, pushing into the circle. We note that each of us has a different boundary where we feel "infringed upon."

Peg tells us that women have smaller circles, even taking into consideration our proportions, than most men. And that women who have been powerfully silenced (abuse, rape, assault, incest) have the most permeable circles and the most difficult time protecting self.

It is important to note, and strengthen, our chosen boundaries.

## MOTIVATION

I was in a group of writers that met for two years to try to collaboratively write a book together. We learned a lot about different approaches to writing, and a lot more about each other. We were a tremendously rich resource for one another, an unlikely group of women. Left to our own devices, we would not probably have chosen each other as friends, yet the process of attending to task blossomed friendship within it.

However, after 18 months, we had copious outlines for our book, and no real writing yet. We had pieces here and there, but we kept losing momentum, then would regain it. It looked like our fire was going out. I asked the question of us: "Let's look truthfully. Do we really want to write?" One woman answered immediately, fervently, slamming her fist down on her leg, saying, "I want to publish."

This startled me. It clearly was true for her. But she had not written much yet. She wanted to edit and pull things together, but the writing motivation was not as strong as the publishing.

Acting coach and author Konstantin Stanislavski, when discussing actors and their art, advises, "Love the art in yourself, not yourself in the art." This applies to writing too. We need to love what Louise Wisechild calls the "I must write" voice in ourselves, not just ourself in writing.

We can be motivated by wanting to publish, to be heard and have audience, students, listeners. This must be balanced with the urge to write because we have something we need to say, even if it is not well received, or not listened to.

And it helps to treasure our craft. Learn it, practice it. Keep working at it until we figure out our voice and what we have to say.

>   Louise:   *It's a test that all writers go through: to devote a lot of time and energy to something and put it out, just trusting that the book will find those who need it.*
>
>   *I was very lucky to get* The Mother I Carry *published, which is the first place that people can get knocked down. To deal with it not being what we think of as "successful" makes me really evaluate, and go close again to that thing that says, "I must write."*

*My work has to have meaning. I have to feel it might help or heal.*

*But the "I must write" voice is the one that reminds me that I write for myself—to articulate my own passions and to survive emotionally.*

It is estimated that only 1% of people at writing workshops and programs are getting published. Students hope that a workshop will result in a magic formula: "If you do this and that, then you're going to get published." Odds are against any single workshop or program resulting in publication.

We need both the inner drive to write and listen and clarify and create—and the desire to connect with an audience larger than ourselves.

For me, finding my own writing voice means being willing to take a stand, to stand apart from the collective and speak up. It sometimes means standing outside of the dominant culture, like Louise's experience, and Yoko Kawashima Watkins' as a child. Or standing apart from our family culture, as Megan's writing required of her. For women, who have experienced marginalization in this culture, standing apart from it again to speak one's truth takes a belief that what we have to say is worth listening to. Or it takes the inner force of having to say it, even if not listened to. When Caroline Bird went to bed for a week, catatonic at an editor's comments on women, and then got up determined to write a book, she knew she had to write it. Even if not listened to.

For women who belong to minority groups, who stand even further outside the dominant culture regardless of gender, coming to voice requires tremendous courage. They are already standing apart. To take another step more, to go on record, requires courage and fire.

## NOW YOU

» How is your writing voice the same as and different from major people in your life?

» Reflect on times when you have been unable or unwilling to write. Were you gathering material, mending internally—what process were you going through?

» What regular disciplines do you naturally have in place? What disciplines do you wish you had in place? Given your personal style, are you working at the level you want and are capable of? What additional support or strategy would help?

# SIX

## *Choosing Voice*

CHOOSING VOICE IS ABOUT APPLICATION: WHEN DO WE SPEAK AND WHEN do we keep silent? What do we choose to give voice to and what do we choose to ignore, or remain silent with? Using our voice is taking a stand, defining ourselves.

In any given situation there are three basic choices: exit, loyalty, or voice. We can leave, disassociate, or remove ourselves; we can remain loyal to the situation, supporting or with silent consent; or we can choose to give voice—and thereby express our unique perspective.

Choosing voice, for me, and for our authors, is about knowing personal values and moral code, and standing up for them.

### USING EMOTION

When a situation becomes intolerable to our own moral code or values, strong emotion can be evoked. Loyalty or exit become unacceptable. Strong emotions can clarify our voice, as we become acutely aware of the stand we choose to take. Listen to Caroline Bird and Yoko Kawashima Watkins.

> Caroline: *I wrote a pretty hot article that said women were discriminated against. Well, the* Saturday Evening Post *turned it down.*
>
> *An editor said, "What Miss Bird doesn't realize is that the really smart women in the offices get*

> *hauled off to the suburbs to have babies. And so in the offices, only the dregs remain."*
>
> *I was absolutely furious. I was so furious that I went to bed, just catatonically for a week. And then I got up and I said, "I will do a book on it."*

Yoko:
> *I came home, Donald my husband of 43 years, was watching "Peter Jennings: Evening News"... when on the screen I saw a Bosnian woman, all the people, and sick, young women pregnant, holding their little child, escaping, some hurt, some crying....*
>
> *All those things made me so angry, I did not know where to throw my anger. I went to a typewriter and I quickly typed ten pages of a story. It is called "Cherry Tree Suns."*
>
> *I was so mad. All those people are still fighting. They don't know what it means to be in that, refugees ... do they have enough blankets? Do they have enough water to drink? Do they have food? Were they cold? How hurt are they? I see myself 51 years ago. That's what I saw on the television....*
>
> *So I got mad. And so I wrote the story, a short story. This will be a picture book.*
>
> *So you see, for me writing is completely healing.*

Writing with voice is a way to make a difference.

### UN-PREMEDITATED VOICE

It was a warm August evening in New York, about 11 p.m. We had all just come from seeing Marcel Marceau's "Last Concert in America" (the first one of several; he changed his mind a few times) and were digesting this visual feast of silent communication, so the crowd was talking softly and going slowly. Except for one man.

This fella had his arm around a glitzy woman. They both were walking with a swagger, and his sarcasm knifed into my awareness: "I'm going to get on the train now, and go home to Connecticut. The little woman will have the kids in bed, and she's going to say, 'Oh, Honey, how hard you work, staying in the office this late, what can I get you?'"

I spun away from my husband and in-laws and right into his face, the words popping out of my mouth before I could censor them in my head: "Oh, no, your wife is no fool. She's home fooling around with your best friend and knows exactly what you are up to." He, and she, stopped dead in their tracks. He stared into my face, to try to place it and remember who I was. He was afraid I knew him. They just stopped right there on the sidewalk, and did not walk any further.

I rejoined my family, walked on, and was greeted with "What made you do that?" It was definitely uncharacteristic behavior, and I had no answer in that moment. But I could not have held those words back for anything. It was a moment of voice, when I had to take a stand. I was compelled to speak on behalf of the woman in Connecticut, setting a backfire to this man's lie with another. It was un-premeditated voice.

In writing, spontaneous words are harder to come by, because their very creation allows reflection. Yet, there are times when voice is pulled from us, when as we write, we find a depth or passion of voice which is unexpected. Knowing when we are comfortable with this, and when we are not, is part of fitting into our own skins, as writers.

### CHOOSING IDENTITY: "REAL" WRITER VS. IMPOSTOR

I was talking with a plucky young woman I know, who was telling me she is a jogger. Now, I admire joggers, since I can't. And I mean I can't. When I ran at an early age, it brought a yelling, scared reaction from parental authorities, so I was trained to walk.

This young woman told me she jogs. "Really? How far?" "Oh, about a mile, sometimes more, sometimes just around the block," she answered. "And how often do you jog?" I inquired. "Two, sometimes three times a week, if I can," she answered.

I was shocked and impressed, both. Shocked, because I would not consider myself a jogger unless I was jogging five times a week religiously, without fail, at least a mile—and then I'd call myself a *beginning* jogger until I could approach three miles. Yet, here she was, claiming this identity outright. I was impressed. In claiming the identity, she could reach her inner standard of "real" jogger with a lot less of a critic around her neck.

For writing, there is a similar issue of legitimacy.

You'll recall in the Preface, I bemoaned not being a real writer:

> *I am a technical writer, and have been for 20 years. But as an author I have been a missing person.*

Megan LeBoutillier echoes this thought and confesses her sense of not being a legitimate writer. Again, I was shocked, because to me, Megan is a "real" writer; she is an author, having published several successful books. "How can you feel this way?" I asked her after the taping. "Same way as you do," she answered. Though I still think Megan is more of a "real" writer than I am, I understood her point.

Legitimacy is in the mind of the standard-setter. What constitutes "real" work, and "real" writing? How much and which voice? What genres? Let's hear from Megan LeBoutillier, Rachel Vail, and Louise Wisechild.

*Megan:* *Even after that manuscript got me a college degree and then was sold and became a book, I didn't think I was a writer, because I still hadn't written fiction. I'd written two books, and I still didn't believe I was a writer. Now that . . . I have somebody who keeps saying "What you do is legitimate writing," I'm beginning to believe I'm a writer. But [laughs] I haven't totally achieved legitimacy yet. In my own mind. But, I'm better. I'm closer.*

*Rachel:* *I kept thinking, "Once [Wonder] is bought, I'll feel like I'm a writer." And then I thought, "Once it's published," and then I thought, "Maybe once my second one is done." And somewhere along the way, I guess, I went to a doctor's office and filled out a form, and under "Occupation," I wrote "writer." That felt like I had declared myself.*

*Louise:* *My critic has this really rigid idea, from school and the structure of the workday, I think, that you have to sit down here for eight hours, or six hours, and if you're not doing that you're not really a writer. I have a friend who actually does do that, and I use her sometimes, I project my critic onto her: "Well, Jenny is the one who writes."*

In the seventies, I took a bus ride from New York City to Los Angeles, a Greyhound special of $75 coast to coast. I was following my father's footsteps; after some college, he hitched to the West Coast and back before he put on the yoke of work. I was also running from the end of a marriage. There were about six of us passengers who were on the bus coast to coast, each with her own stories, which we told each other through the miles. What impressed me was, of the six of us, four claimed to be taking the trip because they were writers. I wasn't one of these. Writing is far too important to me to call myself a writer until I am sure I am a real writer. Until then, I'm a working-at-it writer.

Like British psychologist Melanie Klein's concept of the "Good Enough" mother, I think it helps, however, to make a truce with our critics and agree on what is a "good-enough writer." We need to change our internal critics' job descriptions. See if we can't get our critics to keep watch on: "Am I writing *enough*?" Divert their attention from judgment of our voice, and therefore self, to judgment around the question of discipline, the frame of writing.

## DEALING WITH DISTORTION OF PERCEPTION

We don't bind feet in this culture. But there is some binding of women's voices. This practice is lessening as each generation of women creates opportunities for all women. And as more women are able to use their voices to add their perspectives to the dialogue, to the culture. As a gender, some of us have been taught to give away credit—no bragging, no crowing. We are also sensitive to the group. Since "anonymous was a woman," we sometimes credit others even if the expression is mostly ours.

A study tested the difference between men and women's perceptions of their own achievements. Each gender group took a test and then received their results. The results were rigged, as was the ease of the test: one set of tests was very difficult, and scores were reported low, regardless of performance. The second set of tests was extremely easy and results were falsely reported high.

Then the men and women were asked, "To what do you attribute your performance?" The results were astounding.

For the difficult test, men credited their performance to external factors: the test was faulty, instructions inadequate, not enough time given for the task. Women credited their poor performance on internal factors: "I've never been good at this kind of thing," "I was confused," "I didn't understand the instructions well enough, and should have asked," "I was tired."

When asked about their good performance, men tended to credit their success first to internal factors: "I've always been good at tests," "I like challenges." While women credited their success to external factors, giving their success to others: "You explained it well," "The instructions were so clear," "The test was easy," "Anyone could have done this."

This brings us back to crowing, and finding our true voice. If we've been trained to credit our success externally and debit our failures to ourselves, we're indeed in a bind.

It is important to come to an authentic assessment of our talents and strengths, speaking from our center. When not owning our accomplishments, our voice can feel as if it is hiding behind us, coming from in back. When bragging, it is in front, ahead of us—and can trip us up.

Find your center. Drop down into the belly and speak from your gut.

## THE RULE OF 3

One women's writing group noticed that they tended to present their work to each other with an introduction that diminished, apologized for, or otherwise belittled their offerings. "I'm sorry this isn't finished yet." "You may not like this." "I know it isn't quite right yet."

They decided to limit their critical voices to a "three pot-shots" maximum. The members listened for the self-launched zingers, and called them: "That's one." "Here's two." "Okay, three strikes, you're done."

Then the presenter had to present her work without further harassment. The Rule of 3 in operation is a playful and supportive way to get a leash on our own internal critics.

## INTEGRATING VOICES

Speaking and writing with your own voice does not mean silencing parts, but integrating them. Like the Tibetan monks, who chant with two tones, we do not have to speak in just one voice. Here's Carolivia Herron:

> *Carolivia:* *It is possible not to lose artistic value even when you have many voices.*

We are sometimes pressured to be homogeneous, to be all one mode: all nice, or all pro or con an issue, clear and uncomplex. Yet when I find a personal truth, very often it is a paradox, combining both polarities. Truth inside out. We can love fiercely, and disagree vehemently. So we can write clearly *and* ambivalently, in focus *and* confusion, clearly committed *and* questioning. We can choose to be broad, with texture and dimensions, messy *and* stainless-steel polished.

© Marian K. Henley.

It is helpful to have an accurate inventory of our talents and skills for communicating. Regina Barreca and Yoko Kawashima Watkins bring a richness of material from their inherited voice, merging that inheritance and their own developed talent. We each have our brilliance, where we shine, and our tarnish, those places to polish.

Everybody gets something really perfect, I think. I like people-watching in public places, looking at passersby to see what is their excellence: one who holds a child so tenderly, another who strides with intention and confidence.

Looking at our own writing, it's useful to think about what comes easily and what doesn't work at all, and what can be worked at and improved. Carolivia Herron and Montana Miller comment on this.

> *Carolivia:*    *It is a concept that Yeats had, and he probably had it from somebody else, but his concept was that every writer has what he calls an* automatism, *something you do so well that you'll not even think about it. It just flows out of you, and maybe it is characterization, maybe it is conversation. Maybe it is description.*
>
> *Mine, if I may say so, is description. Give me something as dull as a black pen on a brown table, and I could write three hundred pages.*

> *Montana: I have bad luck trying to make up characters, very bad luck. I hope that I'll get better at this, because I would love to become a novelist, a fiction writer, someday. So far, that hasn't been my best writing, at all.*

## ART VS. CRAFT

There is some lively discussion within these interviews about if and how you can learn writing from a teacher. Caroline Bird expresses skepticism, then off the tape revised her position, saying, *"I think you can teach the craft of writing. The art of writing has to come from within, that cannot be taught."* Talent without discipline is not fruitful, but discipline without talent lacks effective voice.

Boleslavsky begins *Acting: The First Six Lessons*, with his protagonist saying, "I hear that you teach dramatic art." The response:

> *No! I am sorry. Art cannot be taught. To possess an art means to possess talent. That is something one has or has not. You can develop it by hard work, but to create a talent is impossible.*

We can apprentice ourselves to writers, in person or in print, and thereby learn that "something more" that can be transmitted in teaching. Phyllis Hoge Thompson apprenticed herself to Yeats and Rilke, and Carolivia Herron apprenticed herself to Milton's *Paradise Lost*.

> *Phyllis: Two poets have mattered more to me than any others: Yeats and Rilke. I chose Yeats for my doctor's thesis, because I knew that no matter how long the graduate work took, it would be impossible for me to grow tired of him. And I knew that because of the babies [four children], it would take a long time.*
>
> *Even so, after I had been writing poems for some years I still could not tell for sure whether Yeats had affected*

*my own poetry, except that I loved what he wrote, since I very early found out I lacked the power to imitate him....*

*It's harder to talk about Rilke. He is the first person I loved after Yeats. He changed the way I think, the way I write, the way I live. I have lifted lines from his work in each of my three books. And some poems which seem very distant from anything he wrote actually began with him.*

Carolivia: *They said, "What's your favorite book?" And I said to myself, "May my tongue cling to the roof of my mouth if I ever say it's not* Paradise Lost *by John Milton.... May my right hand forget its cunning!"*

*And I just said, "Paradise Lost."... even in a situation where it would not be politic to say that, to admit to it, I could never deny what that book did. It took me out of Hell. When I was eleven years old. And carried me.*

### THICK SKIN VS. STRONG CORE

When you choose voice, you know someone is not going to agree with you. There will be opposition, criticism. There are two ways to deal with criticism: either get a strong thick skin, or a strong inner core.

Regina: *Women need to learn how to get what has often been the private articulate discussion, exploration of emotion and ideas, into the public. We need to be able to do that.*

*It's our responsibility. That means accepting the possibility of failure. We were girls, so we've been*

> encouraged to accept the possibility of failure—failure is not unfamiliar to all too many of us. What really scares a lot of us is that people don't like us. And that's going to happen too.
>
> You open your mouth; someone is not going to like you. And you talk to 20 people, you talk to 50 people . . . somebody's going to get mad, to feel you're bossy, somebody's going to feel you have a big mouth, somebody's going to be upset. And that's okay.
>
> You are not going to make anybody like you anyhow. Why say, "But if I say something like that, they're going to think I'm a bitch. They're going to think I'm trying to take over. They're going to think it's like . . ." And your point is? Yes? Okay, now it's up to you; why do you care?

You may also have to deal with jealousy. When someone is jealous, they try to "take it, break it, or denigrate it." Criticism can originate from jealousy's "denigrate" motivation. Criticism can also come from trying to take your voice, or your spirit, and break it.

## ALLOWING FOR CHANGE

Rachel Vail's "Permission not to have to be Mozart" really resounds for me. I have wrestled with the myth that, to write and let you read it, my thinking has to be fully mature, complete, finished—and that five years from now, I'd agree 100% with what I wrote. There is something daunting about the permanence of the written word. A phone call fades, even e-mail is more likely to be deleted than not. But a written note can be taken out and read over and over again, over time. And it continues to speak from the person who wrote it—who I might not be in five years.

Annie G. Rogers, when talking about writing her memoir book, *A Shining Affliction: Tales of Harm and Healing in Psychotherapy*, said that one of the most difficult tasks in the writing was to go back to the person she was when she was experiencing this, and write from that voice. That's one thing, memoirs. Somehow, change in that genre is expected.

But, for me anyway, I have had to work at giving myself permission to grow in my writing. To begin with a piece that I know I will be able to improve on someday, but let it be read, let it go. I struggle with this concept in writing this book. Roni Natov, a professor at Union Institute & University, told me, "Just do your best writing. It will change. You are still learning and will always be." That helped.

Then I thought about the other arts—specifically, looking at Georgia O'Keeffe's work. Her early pieces, in black and white, are very clearly early efforts with seeds of her later brilliance. Put an early sketch next to a wondrous oil from the end of her career and step back. I can only have admiration for where she began, and where she concluded.

So, I foster my courage and court inspiration by tucking an early O'Keeffe near my keyboard. And give myself permission to grow.

### OWNING OUR OWN VOICE

We have explored the voice we inherited and our own natural abilities, and we have talked about some ways to describe these attributes. We've discussed the process of developing voice, and the act of choosing voice.

We learn from times we have been out of voice, and have not chosen to stand up for our beliefs, or share our perception. And we learn from times when we do. Each of us has a voice range, primary and secondary intelligences and standard ways of communicating.

But what about a definition of voice?

Speaking about the Women's Movement, Caroline Bird said, "Femininity appears to be one of those pivotal qualities that is so important no one can define it." Similarly, voice is a pivotal quality, and no one person can define it. Each of us must define it for ourselves. (Which is why Carol Gilligan's seminal work *In A Different Voice* did not offer "a" definition of voice, I believe.) And voice is additionally elusive to define because it is fluid, impacted by environment, by our own developmental stage, and by the choices we are making by using our voice—by our intentions.

It is powerful to be constantly witnessing our voice, owning it, watching it, choosing how we use it, and seeing what gifts it brings to the human conversation. We can be aware of the impact of our communication on others. We each make a difference.

There is no one "right" voice that all need aspire to. Nor is there a "right" voice for each person—only voice more or less authentic. The more we can each communicate from the fullness of our own authentic voice, the richer the communication.

#### NOT THE FINAL WORD

As in Caroline Bird's interview, which begins the next section of interviews with a range of voiceful authors, this is clearly not the last word, nor the first, on voice. What I hope we've done together is fueled a fuller conversation, and given you some tools and permission to crow, to start squawking and squeaking, to find your own authentic voice.

We need to hear it.

*The Interviews*

# Caroline Bird

*To hell with the opposition—just go ahead*

**GENRE**
Advocacy; social commentary and research

**RESEARCH INTERESTS**
Feminism; social change

**PUBLICATIONS INCLUDE**
*Lives of Our Own: Secrets of Salty Old Women*
*The Two-Paycheck Marriage*
*Born Female*
*The Crowding Syndrome*

Please describe your writing voice.
I am interested in ideas. I try to write so that the idea comes from my head into the head of the reader, as if it was just dropped there and without any sense of any intermediary. What I want to do, ideally, is to state an idea so clearly and so simply that anybody can understand it. That is what I aspire to.

I am interested in the ideas. "Voice": I have a hard time with that business, "voice." If what you are talking about is what we used to call style, I think I was brought up as a journalist and some of my ambition for myself was to be journalistic, except that I wanted to be very good. I wanted to state an idea very clearly with just enough support so that people see it.

I guess your voice changes with the times. I started out with the idea that I shouldn't be in it at all. It should just be a transfer of an idea from my head to other people. But then, I'm not immune to the fashions. Readers seemed to expect that you talk about yourself, so all right, I'll talk about myself. But always in the same way. I mean, simply and clearly. That's what I try, anyway. So it's not like Spenser's *Faerie Queene* that you can always tell who wrote it. I don't aspire to that and don't have it, I don't think.

I don't think that writers really live in worlds of their own—well, everybody lives in a world of his or her own. But if you are interested—and I am interested in writing, I am interested in doing it well, I'm interested in other people who have done it well—I read all kinds of things that I certainly would never write or aspire to write. I think one is affected by that.

*How have you had to defend your writing voice?*
I've said I've had to defend my ideas, oh yes. Actually, I've never had really bad reviews, I can't think of one that is bad. I remember *The Invisible Scar* where there was faint praise. *The New York Times* reviewer said, "She deals competently with events of the Depression, but she doesn't seem to make a distinction between the Federal Reserve Board and the Reserve Bank." And of course he's wrong about that. It was a male reviewer, of course. This was before the women's movement.

My husband (it's like what Roosevelt said about "my little dog doesn't like it, what they say.") wrote a stiff letter to *The New York Times* saying that in fact Caroline Bird *had* made the proper distinction between the Federal Reserve Board and the Federal Reserve Bank. Of course, no reply. That sticks in my mind.

One of my problems is I've often had the first book, of anything. I got one kind of glowing review, and at the end of the review she wrote, "But I don't think she has written the last word on women." Of course, [the reviewer's] own book came out the next year. But that's what reviewers do to you . . . review books with kind of an ax to grind because they think this stirs things up.

But I'm not answering your question. Defending my voice: I don't know that I ever did. But I'll defend my ideas, all right. I guess this business, this "voice," throws me. What I have to say I will certainly defend, and do.

Let's see, I was on a lot of television shows in the beginning, with *Born Female*, with one of these male chauvinists. I've gotten really badly treated by the television talk people. He said, "I see you don't wear a wedding ring." I said, "No, I don't." He said, "What does your husband think of this book you have written?" I had a snappy retort on that. Yes, I got some pretty heavy flak for the ideas in *Born Female*. I managed to hold my own, I think. I try to give back as good as I got.

*How did you pick your genre?*
I wrote all these magazine articles actually for money so I learned how to do that. Diarmuid Russell talked me into doing my first book.

How did I write *Born Female*? How did I become a feminist? People are always asking me this. Really, I was a professional writer, I guess.

I remember being in an Overseas Press Club lunch—my husband loved to go to it—and I happened to be seated next to a guy from the Defense Department. This was during the Vietnam War when they were trying to get people to enlist. He said, "Why don't they have women? Why don't you write something about women in the services?" I thought this was kind of a good idea.

So I got the *Saturday Evening Post*—they had these guest editorials—to let me do a one-page guest editorial, "Let's Draft Women Too." In it I was struck by the fact that most of the jobs in the military were desk and clerical jobs. Women got off scot-free. Actually, I thought it was a good way to get people thinking about the Vietnam War.

It drew an awful lot of attention, of course, all hostile, and that was kind of fun. I've had a lot of hostile attention. I mean, you're just reminding me now. [Laughs]

*You put it out of your mind.*
Yes. Then, the editor of the *Saturday Evening Post* thought this was so ducky that he called me in and said, "Do you think women are discriminated against in business?" I said, "No, I don't think they are discriminated against. I've always been able to do everything I have wanted." I thought this was true.

This is what is a good thing for anybody that is spearheading something: Forget about—just to hell with—the opposition. Just go ahead.

He said, "Why don't you do an article, why don't you spend a little money. Go out and find out how women feel about this." He felt some great idea had struck him. This is 1966.

So I went tearing across the country interviewing women who had gotten anywhere. They were women who were supervisors of telephone operators—all women. They were copywriters for women's fashions. They had dress shops. And the only bright thing that has ever happened to me is that suddenly it was clear as a bell—I had been assigned to this job because I was a woman, you see.

I have always been good on research, like Jim Michener I guess.

So I went to the Labor Department and I discovered this marvelous woman—she is really the founder of the women's movement: Katherine East. She plied me with all sorts of marvelous statistics, how women got paid less than men, and so on. God, she was brilliant. She was the one who discovered that the Xerox machine is a great weapon. She would Xerox documents and send them to people—this was way back in 1966.

I wrote a pretty hot article that said women were discriminated against. Well, the *Saturday Evening Post* turned it down. An editor said, "What Miss Bird doesn't realize is that the really smart women in the offices get hauled off to the suburbs to have babies. And so in the offices, only the dregs remain." I was absolutely furious. I was so furious that I went to bed, just catatonically for a week. And then I got up and I said, "I will do a book on it."

I had one good book out. Eleanor Rawson, the editor I lunched with in the Algonquin [who gave Caroline her first book contract on a handshake], well, her husband owned a publishing company, and she agreed with me. But she was very chary about it. I did the book, and I had a tough time with it too. The ideas were all new again. I remember what she said—Betty Freidan had done this one [book]—she said, "Well, I guess there is room for *another* book about women." (Laughs) Another book!

*Betty hadn't said the last word either?*
Yes, Betty hadn't said the last word, there is something more to be said.
So we finally published it.

My first book was *The Invisible Scar*; my second was *Born Female*. I titled all my books, I must say. The title for *Born Female* came in a conference that we had, in which I happened to say, "I don't see why women should have to do certain things just because they are born female." Eleanor Rawson said, "Click, that's the title." *The Invisible Scar* came to me while I was waiting in a taxi in New York. You know, you're always held up. I thought of that there.

Usually the editor of the book presents it to the salesmen. Eleanor was concerned because her husband owned the company, and it was a book about women in business. She was concerned that they would somehow think it was a self-serving book. So she said, "Why don't you present the book to the salesmen?" This had never been done before. I said, "I don't mind presenting it." So I got up—of course, all of them were men—and I told them what the book was about and why it was important. And by god, they all loved it. Those salesmen went out and sold that book and they kept it in print for ten years.

So, sometimes it's pushing on an open door. I was the first woman to testify before the House of Bishops of the Episcopal Church when they were trying to abolish the women's department. The women had been consigned to a secondary role in the church. And one of the women was chairman of the women's committee, and wanted to present the notion to the bishops that they abolish the women's division and make men and women equal in the church. She asked me if I would come and testify.

[Some] Episcopalians like to say that the U.S. Constitution is modeled on their Constitution, but they happened about the same time. [Episcopalians] have a sort of senate. The protocol is to testify before a sub-committee. I did a good job on that. I really got that little speech. (It was reprinted in *Vital Speeches,* as a matter of fact.) It was kind of straightforward, I minced no words. Afterwards, the Episcopal bishops all gathered around and one was sweeter than the other. They thought I was exactly right. [Laughs] You know, they were just saying that. They were about to do it anyway.

The interesting upshot of that one was that my husband [Tom Mahoney], who is in the public-relations business—that's my notoriety—sent off the speech to *Vital Speeches*.

It is interesting to live to be old because you can see what happens. About three or four years ago, I'm minding my own business when the phone rings and a young man is on the phone and he is doing a Ph.D. thesis. (My god, not only is there "another book on women," but there are Women's Studies. People get Ph.D.'s in it, even men get Ph.D.'s in it. I'm always struck by the proliferation of academia.) So he's doing a Ph.D. thesis, and this thesis is on how the women's movement changed the language.

Well, I never thought I was changing the language. But it turns out that I was the first person to use the word "sexism," at least popularly. I said, "Oh no, I'm not. It was a sociological term." I think I deterred him, because I think that's not right.

I did write it in *Born Female* and I had a copy editor who questioned the term and said, "It isn't in the dictionary." I said, "It doesn't have to be in the dictionary, does it? Writers make the language." So she very acidly said, "All right, but what does it mean?" I said, "It rhymes with racism. It is going by sex where sex doesn't matter." She wrote it right into the dictionary, which was the only way she could let me use this word.

Well, I had forgotten all that. Then in the course of the evolving years, time passes, and three years ago, I get a call from somebody who is doing *A Companion to Women's History*, and it's an encyclopedia. I guess it was Gloria Steinem who suggested me as the person to do the little piece on sexism. But Gloria still thinks it was the SNCC people who used the word first, somebody she knew. I was terribly worried about the priority on this, if it turns out to matter. The fact of the matter is that a word like that can't be ascribed to just any one person. It just springs up out of the Zeitgeist.

So I got Robin Walsh to help me (and she's been working with me ever since) to do real research on it. And, so help me God, I was the first. It was not that the other people followed me. It just happened by accident. It really is because my husband sent this off to *Vital Speeches*.

*What do you call your genre?*
I suppose advocacy. But advocacy implies—I've never joined organizations. An advocate is somebody who founds something like N.O.W., and they head campaigns. All I do is write. I like to state ideas in a forcible way that will convince other people.

How did I pick that? Well, I told you about *Born Female*, how I got into it. I got into it backassed. I mean I didn't start out with an idea—speaking about women being oppressed people. Reporters keep on saying, "What made you into a feminist?" Well, I didn't start out with the idea I was going to be a feminist. I am interested in ideas and where they lead.

And really, that editor of the *Saturday Evening Post* who got me started on this deserves the credit. He did what editors are supposed to do. He sensed that this was something a lot of people are interested in. What he did not anticipate was the force.

When I looked into it I got hopping mad. You see. That's kind of the history of a lot of the stuff I've written. I tend to react to what is happening to other people. I get an idea about it and I follow it and defend it.

*What is your earliest memory of writing or communicating?*
When I was nine I wrote poetry. I mean I've always been writing something. But I never thought that I would be a professional writer and I probably wouldn't have been if I hadn't had to make a living.

People say, "How did you get started?" Well, I tell them, "Would you like there to be a war on?" Because what really happened was during World War II. I was literally drafted onto the desk of a newspaper. I was married by then and had a little girl and my husband decided he was going to the war. This was World War II and he was an engineer and he'd been all over the country building army camps. He could have declined because he had a child. He said, "This is the biggest thing that is going to happen in my life. Other people are getting shot at and I will never forgive myself if I don't go." He went.

And I suppose I never really forgave him. He could have been just as effective [staying home]. He was absolutely marvelous in the war and I ditched him when he came back. Because I guess I felt deserted in a way.

*Did your teachers encourage you in your writing when you were young?*
No, why should I be encouraged by my teachers?

*Sometimes teachers will encourage.*
Well, I went to this progressive school, but I don't think teachers had that much influence on me. My father. Oh, I don't know as anybody ever particularly encouraged me. You see I never thought of myself as being a writer. Although, let me see, I was on the high school newspaper. I was on the [Vassar] *Miscellany* news. It [writing] just seemed like a natural thing to do.

*Because your father was a writer?*
Yes. I read like a fiend. I bored through my father's library, one volume after another. Just whatever happened to be available, paying no attention to what it was. In high school I remember taking a literature course. Oh, I decided when I got to Vassar, I wouldn't waste Vassar on taking courses in English because I was going to read everything

anyway. At one time I thought I'd read everything in the New York Public Library. Because there I would bore right through it. I guess words were natural, but I never thought of making a living by it. Then came the war.

I found once Ed went off to war, I was literally drafted onto the desk of the newspaper. I didn't want to do it and said I couldn't do it. But the copy editor of the *New York Journal's* textile desk editor was drafted. A whole bunch of guys who lived in my building said, "Come on, you can do it. We've got to have someone on the desk."

I said, "I can't do it. I can't do it. I can't do it." They said, "It's easy we'll show you how." I bought a bottle of liquor and they came around and were going to show me but they didn't. They just drank the liquor. [Laughs]

Then I went to work for the *New York Journal of Commerce*. And I was sort of a Fay Henle. A lot of women were drafted on the desk of newspapers. Nobody gave me any help whatsoever except that old Linotype operator—when I had to write or edit stuff like gray goods. Do you know what gray goods are? I'll bet you don't.

*Yes, it is like an old egg carton, pressed onto the Linotype and you could read it. My father set his newspaper in Linotype, when I was five years old. So you know how to do that.*

Yes.
You know who was not supposed to touch type? The compositor that helps get the newspaper out. I would take that copy down there and make it fit. He couldn't touch type because the union wouldn't let him. He showed me how to put your hand on it and turn your hand around and you can read it [gestures with the inside of her arm, pressing into the type bed and then lifting to read it].

*From your arm?*
Sure, it's the same thing.

The first time I brought the copy down, I wore a red dress by mistake. And they shut the lights off. A woman had never come down there, at least a recognizable one, and they started to whistle and stamp. Nobody helped me except poor old toothless Huey who had to get the paper out.

But I learned to write headlines and I learned to write headlines very well. What gets me is that people go to school to learn these things.

*How long did you do that?*
I was there about three months. I was then immediately whisked off to *Fortune*. Want to have a war on? You'll see what it will do for your career. I met Kenneth Galbraith here. Years later, after I was writing for magazines, including *Esquire* (Arnold Gingrich there was a marvelous editor who let me do whatever I wanted), I was assigned to a new editor, Harold Hayes, who spent his Nieman fellowship years at Harvard. And he said, "You know there is a professor at Harvard, I think it's worth a story and his name is Ken Galbraith." I said, "That's interesting, I know Ken Galbraith." So I called up Ken and said, "I have been assigned to write about you." I went up to Boston and I wrote a great story about Ken Galbraith, the first one about him.

As I often say to people, I don't necessarily write the best pieces but I very frequently write the first one.

*What role has silence played?*
Silence! As you can see I don't shut up much. I don't know what you mean.

*Some people have answered it with when they were asked to be silent or people tried to silence them. Others talked about using silence as they write—how they use it.*
How they use it? Well, maybe I should have been silent more often but I don't know as it has been a problem exactly.

*Used it as a tool?*
No, I've never been smart enough to use it as a tool.

I just go off and say what I would like.

*What's been the hardest part of writing?*
None of it is exactly easy. I suppose the hardest part is getting the idea and pruning out the things that don't belong.

*Because you get so many ideas?*
Because when the idea is forming, what you are doing is, you are creating this house. You do it by free-associating and all sorts of stuff comes up out of you and not all of it is going to belong to this structure, to this house that you are building.

Was it Michelangelo who said, it is there in the marble, you just have to get it out? And you do that by getting rid of. You don't think that you are making something. What you think is that it is already there. And that you have to extricate it from all this other junk that's around.

But that is [just] what you think—it is *not* that way. What you are doing is making something that *wasn't* there before. And that, I guess, is the hardest part. You don't wake up and say now, "I am going to be creative."

*How do you know what does and does not belong?*
When you are working on it, you get off on tangents and you get so interested in this, you see [gesturing to a little piece], but that belongs in something else that belongs in another story. That's the hardest part. Of course, that's the essence of the creative process. I don't think about these things much. I just try to do it. I just do it.

# Yoko Kawashima Watkins

*A shout from the heart*

### GENRE
Young-adult nonfiction; memoirs

### PUBLICATIONS INCLUDE
*My Brother, My Sister and I*
*So Far from the Bamboo Grove*
*Tales from the Bamboo Grove*

*Please describe your writing voice.*
In simplicity. A shout from the heart. That's all, nothing more.

Tell the truth, and the feelings.

Also I am a children's writer, so the sentences and the words should be chosen very carefully. You cannot use difficult words. Use simple, simple words that capture the audience. That's about all.

*Has that changed for you over time, how you write?*
It is very difficult for me, because I am an English-as-a-second-language person. I often use Japanese expressions. Still, I can't translate it

directly into charming English. So what do I do? I frustrate. But I do the best of it. I think and walk a little bit, I depend on Japanese-to-English and English-to-Japanese dictionaries. Then if I could not find any words, I just vacuum the whole house.

    There is stress, you see. Stress creating the unwanted energy inside. That is to be released. So what do you do? Maybe you can jog, but in my case, I clean the whole house, vacuum very frantically, and then I calm myself down. And I often do the Tea Ceremony, knowing the way of the Tea. That really calms people down.

*Do you do the tea ceremony with yourself?*
Oh yes. You don't have to have any number of other people, because in each movement there is a deep meaning. You have to be very calm to hold the teaspoons and caddies, and how you hold the water dippers and so on. If you are shaking, or if you are frustrated, or if your mind is in a whirlwind, then you spill the waters, you spill the tea powder, and things like that.

*How old were you when you learned Tea Ceremony?*
We, Ko [her sister] and I and also my brother [Hideyo] too, were sent to a temple for the training. We did not just start to learn how to serve, and how to accept the tea. We learned from cleaning temple corridors, weeding and cleaning for six and seven months. Then we learned to sit still. It started from 15 minutes, and then on to 20 minutes. It is very difficult to sit still for five years old.

*You were that young? Did you study this at the Japanese temple in Korea?*
Yes.

*I saw monks perform the Tea Ceremony and then lecture and answer questions about it at the Museum of Fine Arts in Boston, many years ago.*
Isn't it wonderful?

*Yes, it was quite beautiful.*
I think so too. It has most beautiful virtues.

*To go back to your simple shout from the heart, and choosing simple words. In* So Far from the Bamboo Grove, *though you were choosing simple words, what you were saying was not simple. You are able to speak complex thoughts and ideas without fancy words. So some of that is because you are working in two languages. You also are writing this for the middle school years?*
Yes. I aim for fifth and sixth and seventh graders. It happened at that time, at my age. I was, what? end of the fifth grade? And, Jill, just look at the seventh, eighth, and ninth graders: they are nothing but spoiled brats. Excuse me for saying that. They are, they all say, "I come first." They are not even worried about other people's feelings. Oh, come on now. We were trained to do "You come first, I come later." And they also have to have more things this, and more things that. But actually you don't have to have a lot of things. It's simple as that. We can get by.

You don't need a lot of things. After Bamboo Grove in North Korea, and in Kyoto Japan, we had to leave the warehouse because it was burnt. [Discussed in the sequels *My Brother, My Sister and I* and *Tales from the Bamboo Grove*].

*Did your editor suggest that age group, or did you choose to aim your books to that age group?*
No. I just thought this would be the right time to wake them about the facts of what the world is all about. Middle school age thinks the world is developing around them, but it is not. We have to go along with things. I saw it. And I decided, "Maybe if I tell them . . ."

*. . . how quickly your world can be taken away?*
Also, this was not meant for a book at all, Jill. This was ten pages of a letter that I wrote to the most spoiled brattish American child. And I put all the ten pages in the mailbox. When I put up the flag (on the mailbox), it suddenly hit me why my children did not turn out brattish as she. And, ah, this is the parents' fault. When I decided it was the parents, I learned, "Ah, fifteen years is too late for this child."

*So did you take the flag down and take the letter out?*
Sure, and I filed the ten pages. And I stretched it to the chapter. This was the beginning. Very simple minded.

*You did not begin to be a writer?*
No. Oh no, I wrote that in 1987.

I was a very bad child. I didn't want to go to school, because the teacher called me a liar. The teacher branded me a liar in front of all my classmates, boys, especially, jeered at me, and I had no one to play with. My best girlfriend wanted to play with me. After school, the boys ganged up on her and beat her to pieces, so she didn't want to play with me either. Also, I didn't want to go to school anymore.

*When you lived in Korea?*
Yes.

*And why did they think you were a liar?*
What happened was, I couldn't speak with a voice. My vocal chord was swollen and I just couldn't speak up loud. I was always more whispering. I would speak like this [speaking in a whisper], "Good morning."

Momma and Daddy worried so much [about my voice]. One day Daddy came home with momma and poppa canary birds. Daddy said, "Talk to the birds." And it was my responsibility to care for the birds.

Soon one bird began to trill. It was so beautiful. I was only seven years old. I copied the trills, like this ["durrrrr" with her tongue]. Then the same bird began to trill louder and louder, still so beautiful. So I copied. And soon, like this [makes a sound], and I ran to my mother and said, "I have a voice, I have a voice!" My voice was fresh, and I said to her, "OHAYO! Good morning." Mother was happy.

I ran to the school—remember we had no school bus—I ran two and one half miles. And I burst into the classroom, I was so happy, "Listen to me, *listen* to me, I have a voice." My girl friends were very happy, "Say something!" So I squeezed my voice and said, "Good morning."

The bully came out and said, "How did you do it?"

And I said, "I spoke to the birds!"

He said, "What did you say?"

I said, "When I was changing water this morning, I said to the birds 'this summer I'm going to swim.' The bird came down from the perch and took a bath, a bird bath. See? The bird understands what I said. I can talk to the birds."

And he said, "You liar."

I said, "No, I'm not lying, I talk to the birds."

He said, "Birds cannot talk."

"Well, they can chirp, that's talking," I said. I should have shut up right there, and fought with this bully.

He shouted at me, "Liar!" Like this. So teacher came and it all stopped.

Teacher said, "What's going on?" I said nothing. But Bully stood up and said, "Can birds talk?" She looked at everybody and said, "Well, birds chirp but they cannot talk." And Bully looked at me and said, "See?!" [laughs]

When the teacher says something, that is like a God's law. So when Teacher said, "Birds cannot talk," and Bully said, "Kawashima Yoko said that she spoke to the birds and the birds understood her so well." The teacher looked at me and said, "There are two lies: good and bad. You are telling everybody bad lies. Everybody knows that birds can not talk."

I said, "They do too."

*Good for you.*

My talking back to the teacher wasn't a good thing. I was not a good kid at all. Do you see that? That's how respectable Japanese children were towards the teacher, but I talked back. Because I was jeered by everyone. The teacher confirmed that I lied, so what can you do? I lost all my friends.

When I went to the classroom, I looked outside and thought, "When do I get to go home? I like to play with my mother, and brother and sister. That is much more fun than coming to school." I was absolutely miserable. So I didn't study, you see. I just daydreamed all the time. The report card that semester, I failed. I failed every subject. I was scared to show the report card to my mother.

My mother said, "All you have to do Little One, is sleep well, eat well, and get along with everybody, and be sure you go to the bathroom. That's all you have to do." Mother was not mad at me, so okay I passed the one test. Now, how am I going to tackle my Daddy? My Daddy was a very powerful figure in this household.

*Yes, his absence is very present in* The Bamboo Grove.
Very much so. He was a good daddy, but very powerful. He never screamed, he never spanked us, and he never said mean words. But when he looked at us, and when he calls my name and says, "Yoko," that means he is boiling mad. And that's that. He and my mother are very strange, they never spanked us, no screaming, nothing like that. Lower voice, said once. That's that.

So I took a report card to my Dad. I bowed to him deeply first [laughs]. I bowed and said, "Daddy I have a problem. I don't like to go to school, and I didn't study at all and this is the report card." He took it, he looked at it, he said, "I understand." "I understand," he said. Then he officially sealed my report card and he gave it to me and said, "I know you don't like school, you don't like the teachers, but just look at the blackboard. Just concentrate on the blackboard. Then you'll do better." He gave me the report card back and patted my shoulder and said, "Little One, go at your own pace. Eventually you will succeed."

So I decided to study better for my dad and mom, not for myself. I like my daddy so much, I said, "I will study better."

I took the report card back to the teacher. Teacher opened it, looked at it, and she said, "Are you sure you didn't stamp this yourself?"

*Whoa.*
So I went back to my seat, shoved all my school things in a bag, and I cried all the way home. At that time, shadows of the war were getting so much worse. My daddy was walking in the bamboo grove, head down, hands were held behind his back, thinking, walking, thinking. I ran to him. I was crying. And what happened?

I told him. Always he and I hold hands and walk together. Not that morning. He turned around and took a fast pace to the house. By the time I came to the entrance there, he was already dressed in Western clothes and took off to school.

The next day, I was not going to school. I stayed in bed. Daddy said, "Little One, get up, it is time for school." I said, "No, I'm not going. I don't like school. I like to stay home and listen to mother tell me a story. Its more fun that way." [laughs]

He said, "You have to go to school." I said, "No, I don't want to be teased anymore. I don't want to be called a liar anymore." He said, "No, they will not call you a liar, and you should go to school." I said, "No, I will not go to school, I will not." And I did not go. I was so stubborn, yelling and screaming. I did not go.

Finally Daddy said, "Okay, stay home then. But, you have to learn. I'll give you the homework: write it down. Write it down, what exactly has happened since the birds came to you."

Jill, I was really learning how to print the alphabet. Japanese have a hundred and three alphabet. One hour a morning, I would write in my room with Mother, sometimes knitting, sometimes mending, and sometimes ironing. I would ask Mother how to spell this one, how to spell that one. An hour is over, and we did housecleaning and marketing. If there was some lesson, like calligraphy or go to the temple to do the cleaning for Tea Ceremony, I enjoyed it. In the evening again I would do one hour of the writing, one hour twice a day. It took me maybe three to four weeks, a long time.

When I completed [the story] I showed it to Daddy, and Daddy said, "Make a fine copy." Well, to finish about 50 pages? Ah, that's too much work, Jill.

*For a seven-year-old, yes.*
Because I wanted to play all the time. So I said to Father, "Ooh, this much?" So he said, "Make five full copies." I wasn't going to do *that*, I was too lazy for that stuff. And father gave me manuscript paper. Do you know what Japanese manuscript paper is?

*The beautiful rice paper in scrolls?*
Rice paper with one-centimeter blocks, with 400 blocks. We put each syllable in that block, and the comma, even period, in a block. So the printer will know how many words. I took another week and weeks to do that too. Finally I completed it. Mother was there morning and evening, one hour each time twice a day.

Sometime in the evening she was there cutting vegetables and cleaning the daikons and the carrots and so on. She sat there until I finished one hour. Then Daddy read it, and he put it in a big, big white envelope. And he put an address on top. I thought, "Ah, Daddy is going to send my story to the grandmother in Japan." So we hold our hands and go to the post office.

About three months later, at our house we all sat on the floor and we ate from individual lacquered plates. On Daddy's left was Hideyo and his friends, boys; on Daddy's right was Ko and me and my girlfriend, we are there. Anybody could bring guests. And finally at the end of the table, Mother, to serve us.

At supper time it was just wonderful. Daddy always asked Hideyo [Yoko's brother] about the progress he made. Progress means, he doesn't have to come home with the good grades. Daddy listens to what Hideyo says: "I picked up some strange bug," and we would look at the bug under the microscope, his strange colors, things like that. Simple things.

*And Ko was going to school at this time too?*
Sure. Ko was almost at the end of the primary school, because she and I are six years apart. Ko spoke her piece. And I spoke my piece. I said to Daddy that day, I can still remember, "I learned to write difficult Kanji by studying 'pawnshop.'" And I was proud. Everyone roared at that.

Then Daddy said, "Okay, if everyone has had their say, and no one is fighting, I'm going to tell you a story." And when he said this, I had already left my place and was sitting on Daddy's knees. My little bottom could go right between his legs, you see?

He said, "Listen everyone!" And he pulled out a newspaper from under the cushion. He said, "I'm going to read you a small little story. It is a beautiful story." Then he read aloud: "'Canary Birds, by Kawashima Yoko age 7.'" That was in the newspaper, it took first place in the Primary Section. So I did write from age 7.

Then he said to me, "Congratulations, Little One. See? I always told you to appreciate your teachers and your friends, but you did not listen to me. You don't like them. If it was not for them, you could not write beautiful stories and sentences like this. Now go back to school for more learning."

So that's the way I went back to school. That's all. Writing brought me to the normal life when I was in the dump.

Again when I was 12, and my sister and I were in danger of either starving or freezing to death, * I thought if I could win (a writing contest)—at least the third place, which gave prize money—my sister and I could live at least a few more days. That essay I wrote was again a shout from my heart, and it took first place. We not only lived on it a few more days, we lived several more months. Because Ko managed the money, and she was good at it.

Then I wrote short stories. But when I came to write *So Far from the Bamboo Grove,* again this is a shout from my heart. It took many, many hours.

When you write any stories, I think you have to shout, you have to shout. Instead of manipulating a word, write it as it is, the way you feel. That's the only secret of my writing. There is no secret to it, really.

*How long did you have laryngitis?*
Long time. I still have a rather cracky voice. If I work in a school all day, the next day I lose my voice, because I have to force myself. If the school gives me a microphone, that is nicer.

*Before you talked with the canary birds, it had been years that your voice was soft?*
Yes. It took me a long time.

---

* IN HER BOOK *(My Brother, My Sister, and I),* SHE TELLS THE STORY OF HOW SHE AND HER SIBLINGS SURVIVED LIVING IN ABJECT POVERTY IN POST-WWII JAPAN.

*And you whispered then. Now you shout from your heart with your writing.*
Absolutely.

*The shout part is being very strong and clear in your feelings?*
Things have to be clear, to make them understand what I meant to say. When I finish a manuscript, I do not let just anybody who knows me read it. I give it to a perfect stranger. Then they can say, "What does this mean? What does that mean?" They can give me the most harsh criticism. I like that very much.

*Then you submit it?*
I don't do it so quickly. I keep it, I read it. I put it away a little bit, I read it again. And again, and again. When I am satisfied with it, then I submit it. In my case, it has taken me a long time.

*Why do you like the harsh criticism?*
Don't you like it? Would you feel hurt?

*When I am trying to write from my heart, I have trouble letting anybody read it until I'm sure I have my feelings out. Then if they criticize my writing, fine. If they criticize my feelings, that's harder for me to deal with.*
Sure. I understand. Again, go back to Tea Ceremony. I teach you. Come to our house, then you'll be all settled down. I think that comes in part of growing up, bringing up by the parents. Suppertime we talk about our feelings. It was always Daddy and Mother who brought us from the shell to where we can see the sun and the smiles. And also that's how I was damned by the girls in the schools. That's a difficult time. I wanted to be in their group, but again I was shunned away from them. That's a claiming kind of thing, made me stronger and stronger and a bigger person.

If people are sincere enough to criticize my writing, they must like me very much. That's how I take it.

*Your first book was published in 1986, and from your "Canary Story" until then, did you write the whole time, or were there times you stopped writing?*
From "Canary Story," I wrote "Understandings," the essay when I was 12. Then I wrote about my brother Hideyo, who died. I was already in the United States. I had four children.

When Hideyo died, because we were so close, I went into depression. I cried and cried and cried. I just could not come out from the most darkest, darkest pit. Then one day I decided, "Well, I know the world does not rotate around Yoko. I have to go around the earth. When the night comes, daylight begins, then night again. And day comes. What can I do?"

My friend told me, "You have to go for professional help." Professional help, to the psychologist? I have four kids and I was not working. I was not about to ask Donald for extra money. I could not do that as he was working so hard to push the family front, making house payments and feed us, and clothe us. No, I cannot do that. Well, okay, I'm going to have to do something.

So I brought my memory back as far as I could remember about my brother. I wrote all about him. Good and bad. When I finished it, I sent that Japanese manuscript to Kyoto, Japan, where my brother worked as a teacher. Teachers read it, loved it. Students read it, loved it. And parents read it and loved it. They published the book in my brother's honor.

*That's beautiful.*
When the book came to me, I thought, "Maybe I will translate this book into English so my children will know all about their uncle." So now I depended on the dictionaries and I translated. By the time I finished it, once again, I saw the beautiful beautiful sun, and I was smiling.

Writing is my mental teacher, really. I would not write until I am in a deep down, something I was suffering emotionally deep. Then I pick up my pen and write things down.

*It is your healer.*
Jill, I tell you, you'd love it, what I say. I came home, Donald my husband of 43 years, was watching "Peter Jennings: Evening News." Because I don't hear well, I don't watch television. When on the screen I saw a Bosnian woman, all the people, and sick, young women pregnant, holding their little child, escaping, some hurt, some crying, I saw that on the screen.

I was absolutely tired, exhausted [from a lecture tour and difficulty with a publishing issue]. I look at those Bosnian people escaping to safety. All those things made me so angry, I did not know where to throw my anger. I went to a typewriter and I quickly typed ten pages of a story. It is called "Cherry Tree Sons." I was so mad. All those people are still fighting. They don't know what it means to be in that, refugees . . . do they have enough blankets? Do they have enough water to drink? Do they have food? Were they cold? How hurt are they? I see myself 51 years ago. That's what I saw on the television when I was tired. So I got mad. And so I wrote the story, a short story. This will be a picture book.

So you see, for me writing is completely healing.

*What is the most difficult part for you, in writing?*
Words. Japanese expression, so charming, but it cannot be translated into English.

*Can you give me an example?*
For instance, we have "Jill is a very sweet person and a best friend of mine." I cannot say "sweet." There is no word for sweet. So I have to say, "Jill is a gentle, kind . . ." and I have to put more adjectives, for instance, "the way she makes a move, and whenever she makes a move there is fragrance of irises." Something like that. It is very difficult.

*It is also very rich, to have to translate between two languages. I have a friend who escaped from Argentina a couple of years ago, and she was talking to me about her work—she is studying refugees—and said, "There must be somewhere our work crosses the street together."*

*I love that phrase.* We don't say it that way often, because in this culture, people don't cross the street together too much. Like you and your father holding hands in the grove. People don't walk together like that often. As they do when they do the Tea Ceremony. To walk in spirit. We are all one in Tea Ceremony.

*Is there anything else you would like to say that I have not asked you?*
You are the questioner. I am the answerer. [Big smile]

*Are any of your children writers?*
They are fabulous writers. They can write the thesis so well, and things. They did not become writers. Of course, I was not going to be a writer. I was going to be a mother, which is very important to send balance to kids, well-balance the kids to the society. Not everybody can be a mother, you know.

*Yes.*
So I was going to be a super mother like my own mother. But somehow I kind of fell into this occupation, and it is good. I go around to schools and tell the children, "Wake up, and be humble." Anything else, Jill?

*Oh no. Yoko, I love your story of the birds. It is just beautiful.*
I have the manuscript, but I have to work more on that. I have titled it *Voiceless Dummy*. That's how I was called in the classroom: *Voiceless Dummy*.

*I like the title "I Talk to the Birds." In Tai Chi there is a movement called "walking the bird." I was told this was from a monk who could just walk his bird on his hand without a leash, because he could feel when the bird was getting ready to take off. And he held his muscles carefully so the bird would never leave. When you were telling the story of talking to the birds, I believe the bird understood you were talking to it.*
When I told Daddy about this, he said, "You did not lie." That's what made me very happy about this. If I knowingly lied, I feel bad. He said, "That is your imagination, and Little One, you must never crush and

destroy your good feelings and imagination. Because children's worlds are built on fabulous imagination." He said, "Savor it and treasure it." That's that.

To this day, I never forget the teacher's name, and face, who called me a liar in front of everybody.

That's why it was so interesting, yesterday you said to me, "How could you remember all that?" How can I forget all these faces and names? It is a tender age, seven, eight, and the war happening and eleven, twelve, thirteen, fourteen. You just cannot forget it. It is there all the time.

*It is your talent to remember it so clearly, though. Not everyone can keep it that alive in memory.*
I think if you want to convey the message, you can. I think I am just an ordinary kid who likes to play around. Maybe a special play with the words. That's all.

# Phyllis Hoge Thompson

*Writing as an act of praise*

### GENRE
Poetry; memoirs

### PUBLICATIONS INCLUDE
*The Painted Clock: Mogollon in the '80s*
*Letters from Jian Hui and Other Poems*
*The Ghosts of Who We Were*
*What the Land Gave*
*The Serpent of the White Rose*
*The Creation Frame*
*Artichoke and Other Poems*

*Please describe your writing voice.*
That's hard. I think it's personal, it's musical. I suspect it's the same as my speaking voice, because people recognize me speaking on the telephone very readily, so I think that what I have done is to reflect my speaking voice. I think my voice is somewhat formal. I'm not afraid to use inverted structures, for example, and I know my voice is also correct, as I'm a grammatical stickler, so there we are.

*What do you mean by inverted structure?*
Placing words into a structure where they are not usually expected: "a bright bird / wind-stalled." *

Inverted structure also happens to be Hawaiian—for instance, "*kolohe, ka ilio*" means "mischievous, the dog"—and I'm certain that the Hawaiian mode of speaking has influenced what I have written.

*How long did you live in Hawaii?*
Twenty years.

*How has your writing voice changed over time?*
I became more confident of my ability to say what I wanted and not worry about whether I was going to have the ability to say it. I began feeling as though I could say it—whatever I wanted to say, I would find the right words. My poems became less imitative—far more my own. It just happened.

I gave a reading last night at the University of New Mexico from earlier books, and it was quite interesting to me to see some of the things that I did a long time ago. I could almost cite the writer that I was imitating. At one point last night when I read "Waiting for Snow" from *The Creation Frame*, I felt very strongly the influence of Rilke there. I probably was quite aware of it when I was writing that poem.

I think now that the imitations, or the words that I respond to from other poets, fit more naturally into the poems. You would hardly notice they're there, unless you happen to know the poems they come from.

*I just popped open "Waiting for Snow" to read it:*

> *White of ash is the light bark of the trees that are waiting*
> *For snow*
> *(Ash color on the charred sky of winter)*

---

* From "The Day of Change," in *What the Land Gave* (Quarterly Review of Literature Poetry Book Series).

*With a stillness so absolute
That they, who are strong, seem frail. . . .*

Yes. A young man asked me last night, why did I use parentheses, around the third line. I was thinking that over today, and I guess I'll write and tell him that I think what that shows is a kind of surprise. When I put parentheses, I mean: wow! [Laughs] I think that's what the parentheses do, emphasize and surprise.

*A kind of awe?*
Yes.

*Have you had to defend your writing voice?*
No, I don't think so. I can't imagine having to. It simply is.

*How did you pick your genre of poetry?*
I never had any choice. It just happened. When I was about four years old I began talking poems, my mother wrote them down, and when I could write them down myself, I wrote them down.

*You began talking poems?*
Well, yes, I guess, making remarks, yes. That is how she described it. And certainly by age six I was writing by myself.

*Then when you were in third grade, you wrote that you were given the poetry prize in an all-school contest.*
Yes, much to my astonishment. To be recognized by someone—Babette Deutsch I think, or maybe it was Louise Bogan—someone, anyhow, who knew what she was talking about said that, among the three winners from the twelve grades, I was the one who was a poet! I think that was remarkable of her, to see it so early.

When I look back at the poem I wrote then (as if it were not mine but some other child's work), what I can see is a clear and strong sense of the rhythms of language, and of a free way of approaching the subject. I wasn't afraid to write about something even if it happened to be of epic proportions. [Laughs] And I also was writing not personal confessional stuff. I was writing about something that mattered and was of interest to me. And I think that that's probably what the poet picked up on.

*What was the epic proportion that you were writing about?*
I was writing about figures of the *Volsung Saga*. We were reading the *Volsung Saga*, if you can imagine, and I wrote about Siegfried, and didn't seem to be afraid of the heroic subject. Maybe because we were young, it was natural to write about things that we cared about. I had a wonderful school.

*Yes, for the third grade, that's very progressive.*
In third and fourth grade we were doing *Jason and the Golden Fleece*, and the *Odyssey*. We had a really fine teacher. It was just a stroke of luck, of course—you never know when you're going to get one. Miss Esterly. She taught both third grade and fourth grades together in the same room.

*Have you ever wanted to write anything other than poetry?*
Yes, and I've tried, recently. There is a superb teacher here this year at UNM (the University of New Mexico), named Sharon Ord Warner. Last fall I took a course in fiction writing from her, and she is really remarkable. I have learned things from her that I hadn't been able to take in before. I'm catching on, I think, to fiction. I would like to write some fiction.

*You have taught for many years, and yet here's a teacher who is striking something new in you?*
Yes. I know how to teach poems, I'm sure I do, and the reason I know how is that I write them. So I know how to face the problems and how to overcome them, I know what they are. I know all that stuff. What I don't know is how you do the same thing in fiction. It's a whole other ball game; it's not at all the same.

You're dealing with scenes and characters within another kind of structure from poetry. What I can use, of course, in the writing of fiction is my sense of language. Putting the words together on the page is easy for me. But it's the other considerations that Sharon has really enabled me to understand a whole lot more about than I ever did before. I was very impressed with her.

*And she had your class writing a lot?*
Yes, we wrote at least three stories, and criticized them all. Ordinarily, what you get in a creative writing fiction class, or even anybody's fancy workshop that you pay $150 for, is some teacher leading the group of students in critical evaluation of the work. That is good, but it is not enough. It seems to me that it's a rare teacher who can really give you clues as to how to go about it. Sharon is really remarkable. I think she's published a book of stories relating to AIDS. I think her first or second novel is also coming out.

*What is your earliest memory of writing or communicating?*
The earliest specific memory I have is when I was eleven years old. There was a series of philharmonic concerts, and they had a contest for kids, to write something about the music, to demonstrate music appreciation. So I went to all the concerts, and I wrote my music appreciation. I wrote a long poem about music, how music is present in nature. I was very conscious of having chosen the words in doing that. I won first prize, but not because I understood anything about music but because I knew how to write about it. So that was actually inappropriate, and I realized the judges were rewarding the wrong thing.

*Because you wrote musically about music?*
What I did really was not an exercise in music appreciation, although I know that the judges thought it was.

*Because your piece was so musical?*
Because what I wrote was musical. It was a scrapbook about the five concerts, and it contained a poem and I probably drew a picture, but it had nothing to do with the music. [Laughs]

*What role has silence played in your writing?*
Good question. A lot, I think that's where the poems come from, the interior listening. I used to write down things almost as soon as they happened, but I kind of wait, now, until silence gives me something. And when I give a reading, people are surprised at how long I wait between stanzas, or sometimes even lines, because I think it takes time to assimilate the meaning and music of poetry.

*Is this influenced by your Quaker faith?*
Yes, I think so. Let me read this to you. I happened to have my third book in my hands yesterday, *What the Land Gave*. It's five books published together by the *Quarterly Review of Literature* series.

Each poet was asked to write something about his or her poetry, which is presented at the end of the selection. So, this is going to take about five minutes, maybe less.

[Reads from the book*:]

"I have cared about words for as long as I can remember. My mother fostered and fortified that love. My mother read poems to me before I could read them to myself, and she put the right books into my hands while I was still very young. As a consequence, by the time I was twelve, I had played with every metrical convention and rhymed stanza form described by whoever wrote the narrow red book I trusted. My mother also took me to poetry readings. I remember hearing before the Second World War Robert Frost and Carl Sandberg read their works in a Newark theater.

"I was also very lucky in my school, Vail Deane in Elizabeth, New Jersey, where I learned about the *Volsung Saga* in the third grade, and Odysseus, Heracles, and Jason in fourth, and in the fifth, I acted in the *Second Shepherd's Play,* a part I can still recite lines from.

"Two poets have mattered more to me than any others: Yeats and Rilke. I chose Yeats for my doctor's thesis, because I knew that no

---

* THIS PIECE WAS PUBLISHED IN THE PRIZE-WINNING BOOK *What the Land Gave*, VOL. XXII OF THE QUARTERLY REVIEW OF LITERATURE POETRY BOOK SERIES.

matter how long the graduate work took, it would be impossible for me to grow tired of him. And I knew that because of the babies [four children], it would take a long time.

"Even so, after I had been writing poems for some years I still could not tell for sure whether Yeats had affected my own poetry, except that I loved what he wrote, since I very early found out I lacked the power to imitate him. Later on I decided it was because of Yeats, and because of his theatrical sense, that I got into the way of imagining the place where the poem is happening, what time of day or night it is, and what kind of weather, and who the person is I'm speaking to. That's what's in my mind before the poem comes, and that's from Yeats.

"It's harder to talk about Rilke. He is the first poet I loved after Yeats. He changed the way I think, the way I write, the way I live. I have lifted lines from his work in each of my three books, and some poems, which seem very distant from anything he wrote, actually began with him. "Ka Hea,"* for example (one of a series about voice, by the way, called *Voices,* in which I acknowledge the voice of seven different creative influences), came as a response to "On the Verge of Night." I now teach the *Duino Elegies* in all of my advanced poetry courses, because I believe he is the one poet whose vision will matter critically to the lives of my younger contemporaries. The truth is I no longer know how to write without at least thinking of Rilke.

"It seems to me it follows quite naturally that I think of work as prayer, of writing a poem as an act of praise, of myself as a religious poet. Worship stands at the center of my daily life. I have always been a churchgoer. I began Episcopal. The wonderful language of the *King James Bible* and the *Book of Common Prayer,* which to my ear new translation has made dull as newspaper, was not all, but it was much. It was strong evidence of how the gift has been returned to God the Maker. But I changed. I began to think of poems as coming less from outer event than from inward listening for light.

---

* "Ka Hea," in *What the Land Gave.*

"I became a Quaker. The truth I found in silence began to matter more to me than the truth revealed in the beautiful words of others. My poems also changed. Although I knew they were rhetorical constructs, I wanted to simplify their language to make it more like the truth, which is as simple as it is hard.

"When I write, when I think a poem is ready to come, I sit still for hours waiting for it to gather slowly and speak to me. After the waiting in silence comes the writing, which I love. I love figuring out which words sound truest and best. I love how they fit into a line or a sentence or a phrase. I love their weight; I love all they assemble of thought or feeling. What they remind me of apart from what I have chosen to say. I love how they're spelled and where they came from. I love working out in lines their music, which is for me very securely based in the old-fashioned metrics I learned before I grew up. I love fitting everything together, and I love finding out what the poem says when at last it feels right.

"Whatever my poems mean in particular, they begin and end as celebration of the world entrusted to me by my life. Poetry—my own and that of others—helps me to understand how things are for me, and to live more peaceably with what I have. It is my common prayer."

*That's beautiful.*
Well, I think it covers a lot of ground as succinctly as possible, which is why I read it to you.

*Yes. It's both process and voice and the ancestors of your poems, as well as motivation and purpose—it's very whole.*

*What has been your nemesis or brick wall, the hardest thing for you in writing?*
It's a question of time, I think, largely. When I was having babies I just didn't have time to write. As soon as I stopped having babies and finished my Ph.D., I started. I think time has been a critical matter. Well also, this cancer I have had—it's time out. I mean, I wasn't busy having cancer, I wasn't even thinking about that, but it's sort of always present when you're in the middle of getting cured. Consequently, I have not written much of anything (in the past 8 months). I'm ready to write.

Right now, I'm going to be back in my own house for a while. I don't foresee going anywhere. And that's the first time in two or three years. Although I've done some writing in the past three years, whenever I've been to Yaddo or some other artist's colony, I've been able to pour myself into the work. Now I think I can do it at home, because I can see some time ahead of me. Is that what you mean by my brick wall?

*Yes, that's currently your challenge in getting to the writing. For some other people the challenge might be coming up with characterization. It's whatever is tough for you.*
Well, I can say that it's tough for me to come up with the fiction. And I want to do that. I think I'm learning, because of Sharon. So, there we are.

*When we talked before you mentioned how you begin a poem?*
Yes. It doesn't always happen the same way. Sometimes I begin with a phrase or a line—but ordinarily, I tend to make a kind of a rainbow or arc of words across the top of the page. I have no idea what their relationship is, just words that I feel like bringing forward at that moment, and they kind of scatter across the top of the page and down the side margin. Then I begin the poem. And most of the words I use in the poem. It's a very funny thing.
    An interesting parallel: A. S. Byatt wrote a book called *Possession: A Romance*, which won the Booker Prize. There's a character in it, a man who is a kind of historian, who is trying to get some kind of article out, and to teach. Little by little you can see him turning into a poet, and what he does is to write words in the margins of the paper and on the top of the sheet and down the other margin.
    I was recognizing that, and thinking, isn't that amazing? Somebody else does the same thing! It was quite surprising, the fact that somebody else even knew that that's one of the ways that you start a poem. It was really interesting to me.

*You know, from the time that I met you until about two or three months after that, I was searching for a word for you. And I found one—or it found me: Fulgurant. It means "sparkling-like, and dazzling, like lightning." When I met you, the light jumped, like someone lighting a match. You were just sparkling! And I kept thinking, there's got to be a word for this, or adjective.*

*Then I found it on a piece of paper, that someone had torn off from a word-a-day calendar some year before and it reappeared as I was going through things. So it's your word.*

Well, that's kind of nice. I like that. That's a gift. Thank you.

Yes, well, it's coming back, it's coming back, the energy. I'm just so grateful, because I was doing so much sleeping because of the cancer. You know, "Where has all the energy gone?" Well, I guess cancer does kind of take it out of you. But recovery is well on its way. It wasn't even chemotherapy, it was radiation, and I didn't understand how debilitating that was. But I do now. Oh boy! Do I now.

*Are you going to write about that?*
I doubt it. Years ago, someone collected a group of poems in a book about breast cancer called *Her Soul Beneath the Bone,* and I wrote the introduction. That was enough. I don't need to write anymore about cancer. It was not a deep psychological experience for me, and I did not feel that I was encountering death. My only question was, "Why am I not taking this more seriously?"

My radiation oncologist was a real winner, but she seemed slightly insulted that I was plain not interested in cancer.

*Do you think that you might not have been taking it more seriously because of your faith? I'm wondering if the cancer didn't rock you because you have such a foundation.*
Yes, I just don't feel interested in paying attention to "suffering." It is boring. Now, I may die within the week, but it doesn't feel that way. So, yes.

*Is there anything else that I haven't asked you that you would like to say?*
I think that something that comes up is the question of children, doesn't

it? For all but male writers, maybe them also? I'm very grateful that I had children, and grateful that I have grandchildren. I think that having children turns women outside of themselves, so that although they of course write from their own experience, limited, whatever, so they're less likely to be confessional and centered on the self, the more they appreciate the lives of their children.

This is not something I was able to do in the beginning, but I think I do it more now. I feel much more a part of my children's lives, much more interested in them as people, which is not to say my own life is over, because for sure it isn't, but I feel really interested in them. This is a crazy generalization—that mothers have to become less self-centered as they grow older, and I think that when you become less self-centered you can deal with problems that occur to people other than yourself. You can deal with them honestly. Maybe in a sense that's not writing from one's own experience, but . . . I do not consider my work confessional.

*In my experience as a mother, I needed to become not self-centered but child-centered. And then as the child grows older, there begins to be time again for self and a return to a wider world.*
Yes. But it seems to me that it follows from the fact that initially your self is taken away from you. You have an experience in which you can't devote yourself to yourself. So that you're open to more. Which forces you to look away from yourself toward others.

When you come back, to having time, to explore who it is you are . . .

*You've popped your kernel. You can never go back into that little shell.*
Right. You're much more open, I think. And you can write with interest and attention to things outside of yourself, it seems to me.

*I took a course on cross-cultural healing, and one of the things that was said was, in one of these cultures women when they had children were not allowed to be healers, because if they had that capability, it was to be turned first to their family. And then when they finished with their family, they could go back to the healing work again. So they would often train in the herbs and in the medicines, and then have their children, and during that time they wouldn't work, and when they came back from that, when the children became between eight and ten years old, then they were allowed to return to healing.*

Yes, and something has happened in the interim. You're not a teenager anymore, in love with some man.

*Yoko Kawashima Watkins talked about mothering also, and she said that she did not intend to be a writer; she intended to be a mother. And she also said, it's very important to balance the children to the culture. In her writing, she's doing that with a wider audience. That's why she's chosen the middle school to talk to. So she would agree with you. Anything else?*

I don't know anything else. [Laughs]

[Postcard received two months after interview] Jill—Here's the last word . . . that "voice" question still troubles me. Because one assumes different voices as one assumes different characters. Sometimes I'm crude, sometimes elegant, sometimes funny, sometimes wrenchingly serious. And so on. My style, though—I try to achieve simplicity (one of my mottoes is "Simplicity is an achievement") as well as music of language. I consider my work "formal," traditional. Got that?

Love, Phyllis

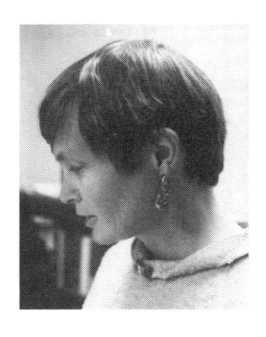

# Joan Hiatt Harlow

*Talent is one thing, and the drive to express it, another*

### GENRE
Early childhood; young adult

### PUBLICATIONS INCLUDE

*Shadow Bear*
*Star in the Storm*
*Joshua's Song*
*Great Molasses Flood*
*Shadows on the Night Sea*
*The Dark Side of the Creek*
*The Creatures of Sand Castle Key*
*The Wishing Sky*

*Please describe your writing voice.*
The child within me still awakens to the word "wonder." I love the sense of wonder that I recall as a child with the newness of things and discoveries. Among my favorite words are "wonder" and "discovery." I especially like being on the side of people, animals, medicine, science

that are controversial but make sense. I don't like establishments or academics that create a fear of change or don't recognize potential. I hate the expression "It can't be done." My writing is usually inspired by my own sense of wonder, including the stories or settings that are unusual.

When I was growing up I felt "different" and would get engrossed in discussions that other people didn't understand or weren't interested in. They would roll their eyes—and they still do. Just last summer I saw my friend's husband roll his eyes to another person about me. It's okay. I used to become defensive.

One day when I was in my twenties I read "The Star Splitter" by Robert Frost. The poem is written in first person and it's about a neighbor, Brad McLaughlin, who loves the stars and wants desperately to own a telescope. He finally burns down his barn and after collecting the insurance, promptly purchases a telescope. The townspeople roll their eyes—or at least that's the way I envisioned the response. But Brad would take people out to split the stars with his scope, which he named "The Star Splitter."

The narrator recalls "a night of broken clouds" and the mud melting, then freezing underfoot. Brad (and the narrator) look up the brass barrel of the Star Splitter—velvet black inside—to a star "quaking at the other end, and standing there until the day broke, said some of the best things we ever said." That poem gave me a sense of freedom and release.

This is the kind of voice I hope to portray to children — that it's okay to wonder, to question and express how you feel. There is still mystery and discovery and adventure, and it's okay to be excited about it. When kids reach "cool" they are afraid to show that sense of wonder. It's almost embarrassing for them. Peer pressure is a real problem for kids.

My book *The Mysterious Dr. Chen* deals with peer pressure and a sense of freedom when the protagonist is no longer afraid of other people's opinions and finds joy inside himself.

One of my favorite prayers for myself, that I read somewhere once is: "God, grant me an open and receptive mind. Restore to me my capacity to wonder."

My stories are based upon unusual, historical, and sometimes controversial things—like the mysterious stone chambers and monoliths in the Northeastern U.S.A.; ocean fossils on mountain tops; ancient religious rites which are still part of modern society, including sports, holidays, the language of flowers; the wonderful healing of herbs; animals that have been maligned and almost wiped out by ignorance and religious superstition. I can probably think of more, but these are just a few off the top of my head.

*How did you feel different growing up?*
I asked so many questions and they were questions people didn't know how to answer. I was a bright child. And I would sometimes put the teachers on the spot about things, some of the things they would talk about.

To give an example: they were finding the frozen woolly mammoths and I was very interested in glaciers and fossils. So I asked what happened to the dinosaurs, which is still a question that's in the air. The teachers would frown when they'd see my hand go up. And I'd say, "Well, what happened to them?" and of course they said, "What we think happened was that there were glaciers and the glaciers moved slowly and the ice age may have killed them." I asked, "How long did it take for these glaciers to move down and kill the dinosaurs on the North Pole or wherever they were coming from?" And they said, "Oh, probably a couple of inches a year." I thought that was very strange and I said, "Why didn't they walk away?" It seemed a logical question to me. But I was told to be quiet.

I began to think, instead of resenting it, that there was something wrong with me. You know what I mean? I don't know if other people feel the same way. Precocious, you know.

*How has your voice changed over time?*
The audience is getting older. I'm now writing for young adults. The stories for younger children are fun, but I have more to say now. Also, I like writing for older kids because I become more closely involved with the more complex story characters.

*How did you pick your genres?*
I guess they picked me. They are the genres in which I have interest and find joy, mystery, wonder, and discovery.

*What is your earliest memory of writing?*
I wrote a story in second or third grade about a wounded bird that I took care of until it could fly. The teacher called me to her desk and told me, "This couldn't happen. The bird could never fly again." I tried to explain that it was a "make-believe" story but I ended up feeling as if I had told a terrible lie. I guess she didn't know about "that willing suspension of disbelief which constitutes poetic faith."

Later when I gave her a poem I had worked on at home, she didn't believe I had written it. But other teachers did recognize my writing abilities and were really encouraging, later.

*What is the role of silence in your writing?*
My mind is always full of turbulence and words and sounds. It's hard to be silent. But I can concentrate very deeply, so when I don't try, I am able to turn off other thoughts.

I need silence and find that if I can let my mind be silent, answers come to me. This is true of my stories when I reach an impasse. When I'm silent and alone and turn off the turbulence, I will "hear" the answer and the plot problem will fall into place. I know that "there's always a way" and to "sleep on it." The answer always comes through the silence.

*What is your brick wall, your nemesis in writing?*
The most dangerous nemesis for me is *obsession*. I've come to believe that when I obsess over a manuscript, something gets hung up "in the atmosphere" or something gets blocked or hits a stonewall. Then a manuscript comes back rejected and I can go into a tailspin; it makes me ask myself, "Is it worth it?" Or "Perhaps all my other successes were flukes." Rejections can be ego-shattering. That's all part of the obsession.

But when I truly let go of a story, good things seem to happen.

This might sound superstitious, but I'm not a superstitious person. This is real—just like sleeping on a problem and finding the answer in the silence.

*Is there anything else you'd like to add?*
If my own philosophies can be summed up in slogans, the following are those that would describe my inner voice: "There's always a way." Yet conversely: "When in doubt, don't." Also, "Sleep on it." And: "Let go and let God."

*What happened at home when you asked questions?*
My parents were very supportive of my intelligence. They would answer my questions or they'd get me books. Although I probably didn't tell them about what was happening in school, like the poem I wrote.

My father was very proud of that poem, but when I brought it to school, the teacher did not believe I wrote it. That was my early recognition; I was probably only six or seven.

I was searching for a word and I used a thesaurus to find a word with the proper beat, the proper rhythm, so that it would work in that poem. The word was "cause"—"the cause of truth." The teacher felt that that was not my writing. So, I never told him [my father]. I felt, I felt . . . silenced. I never fought back.

I wish I could go back. I'd be different.

*But you didn't stop writing? Your writing became private, sectioned off from school?*
Yes. When I got into junior high and high school, I was writing in classes. The teacher in one class asked us to write a story in the first person, an anthropomorphic story. So I wrote about a violin. I wrote from the voice of a violin that was in a Parisian attic and how it was recalling the joys of earlier days and so forth.

Whenever there was a story to be written or theme, when they picked, "who should we have to read their story first," they'd always say, "Let's hear Joan's story first." Which made me feel good because I really loved the power of words. I really, really felt a sense of fulfillment in being able to share this. So this particular violin was in the attic. I did historical research on it, to make it right.

*How old were you?*
I was probably a sophomore in high school. This particular story ended that the last faint glimmer of hope for this violin to be restored or brought out of the attic faded when the owners of the house had gone up there to find things to sell to the rich Americans. They looked at the violin and they said, "Just an old violin" and tossed it aside. But they did not see the writing "carved on my chest through the dust: Antonio Stradivarius." I was what, 14?

I think it was a good story, I enjoyed it. I loved it. It was a joy to do it. I loved writing stories for school. The teachers recognized it, I think.

*When you say, "They said, let's hear Joan's story first," are these your classmates or the teachers?*
The classmates. Right. And then one time, one of the teachers said, "Nobody will want to read after that story." They were kind of spellbound, which made me feel even better.

*You became resilient in your writing even after the teacher who tried to squash you when you were young?*
Yes, the drive to write is stronger than the fear.

Even today, when I get a rejection, it's an awful feeling that comes over me sometimes. Sometimes I just throw the rejections aside and ignore it, send it out again. But sometimes when it's really something important to me or I obsess on it, I've got to be careful of that. I think, "Is this all a fluke? Maybe I can't do it."

I voiced this to a writing friend of mine the other day about one of my books that just came back. I don't think the publishers read it because I could tell it was just too neatly arranged. My friend scolded me on e-mail. She said, "Joan, after all this time, you know, we all feel this way."

No matter how many years you've written or how many successes you've had, you're so personally involved with some of the stories that it's shattering. I can't explain it. But I get over it. I don't quit. Within a few days even I'll send that story out again or get over it anyway. I don't know why. As I said to my friend on the e-mail, "Why do we push ourselves through this? Is it some sort of self-torture at times?"

*Did you come up with an answer?*
I believe in the story. Characters are so real to me that it's almost as if they must live. Perhaps that's it. I'm very close to this particular story that was just sent back. It is in a contest now at my other publishers. If it doesn't win or get published through her, I'm going to camouflage it with a new title and change the protagonist's name.

Many of my friends who've read the story—they love this story—say, "Oh, you can't change her name." And I thought, no, this is really her, her name is really Nova. And she's an astronomer. She's 16 and already has her master's degree in astronomy.

I'm personally attached to her and in a way, I think it's because I've always been interested in astronomy myself. She is kind of put down in the story. Maybe I relate to her on a personal level. So when that story's rejected, I feel more of a rejection. She is me in a way at a young age.

*Does Nova connect with "The Star Splitter" poem?*
Yes, she does. You know, I found that interesting as I thought about your questions. It brought out things I had not thought about myself.

*. . . Like the Star Splitter poem?*
Yes. That I recognized how freeing that was, I could see but I hadn't thought about Nova being me clearly until I worked on this for you.

I have another story, *Star in the Storm*, a novel about a girl and her dog in 1912 Newfoundland. You may be interested to know that I tried submitting one chapter and a synopsis of this story to my then editor of 20 years ago. When it was rejected I was so ashamed and downhearted that I put it in a drawer and never looked at it again until three years ago. When I found it, yellowed with age, the tears streamed down my face, and I knew this was a wonderful story that needed to be finished and told.

I've been delighted to receive a number of awards for my stories. For instance, *Star in the Storm* has won the ASPCA Award, the Disney Adventures Book Award for Best Adventure Book of 2000, and is an ABA Kids Pick of the Lists. *Star in the Storm* is dedicated to my mother, who was a Newfoundlander and who "sang me the songs and told me the tales."

My daughter, Lisa, and I went to Newfoundland a few years ago, and my cousin took us out to Beachy Cove—a secluded place with cliffs and unusual rock formations, etc.—and I took one photo of him down in the water in his boat. I was on the cliff, and his boat looked so small in the picture. I took pictures of the cliffs and rocky shores. And icebergs!

In my story, a little girl goes out to chip ice from the iceberg for her sick and fevered cousin. This actually did happen many years ago.

The editor sent pictures to Wendell Minor, one of the top illustrators in the country, and he used some of the pictures for reference as he painted the background. Simon & Schuster went all out for *Star in the Storm*. The black Newfoundland dog on the cover is beautiful.

*You said that your genre is changing and you want to write more for young adults because you have more to say and you become more closely involved with the more complex characters. Can you say more about that?*
Well, writing for children who are really young—*Shadow Bear* is kindergarten to grade 3—is not easy. Teachers will say, "When are you going to grow up? When will you write more important things?" "What's more important than children?" I say.

Writing a K-through-3 picture book is not a simple task. It's harder than most people can imagine. You must choose the right words, the right sentence structure. It's like poetry, though not in verse. You have to be very concise and very careful about choosing the correct word rather than a lot of words, so that a child can understand and visualize.

With the older genre that I am writing for now, the stories are more complex and I can address more issues than I could in a young child's book. *The Mysterious Dr. Chen*, for instance, is for middle-grade children, and in it, I address issues of peer pressure, destruction of animals, and ecology.

In one story, a boy wants to be a figure skater and does not want his hockey team to know. The end of this story gives you the goose bumps. The boy decides to figure skate, but has a mask on. The audience is not sure who is skating. This is written in the first person—the boy laughs and feels free. He skates a double axel. Then he removes his mask and surprises even his mother who did not know he was taking figure skating lessons because she is a single parent. He was taking lessons after school using his newspaper route money.

I think peer pressure causes a lot of the drug abuse—trying to be cool; trying not to show they like certain things. And parents are responsible by saying, "That's a dumb question" or not communicating on the right level to kids.

*How does a story like that become alive in you?*
It starts in a small way and often grows. I originally started this story as a magazine story. Then it grew.

We have a summer place on a lake in New Hampshire. And we had trouble with bats. In fact, we couldn't even eat dinner in the house without a bat swooping down. We learned they had taken over our house as their house. It was the talk of the neighborhood children. They'd be disappointed if they did *not* see a bat.

When my mother-in-law was about to visit, I warned her about the bats. I had to convince her that I did want her to come up and there truly was a problem with bats. She came up and there was not a bat to be seen. But when she went back to Vermont and opened her suitcase, a bat flew out of her suitcase.

Another time, when we were living in Wilmington and had gone back home, I told my husband I was so relieved not to hear that flutter of wings. Even hearing bird's wings outside gave me goose bumps. After a while, I got up from the sofa and left the room, though he did not notice. He turned to talk to me, and where I had been sitting on the couch, there was a bat.

So I began to learn about bats. I still cannot look at a bat and think it is cute. Yet I understand their value. And it ended up that this time of the bats was one of the best times of our lives.

In the story I wrote, the kids are having a party and a bat flies into the house and they all laugh. There had been some talk about vampires but this story showed how this myth has destroyed innocent animals.

We had so many kids trying to chase a bat out of the house that it looked like one of those mini cars where 40 people get out but it was our house.

*Do you submit through a literary agent?*
No, I don't. Many of my well-known author friends will say, "I'll do it myself." Once established, they go to that publisher a lot. The publisher likes a successful author to continue too.

What I have done is to go through the educational arena. *Shadow Bear* was published by Doubleday. At that time my mother, who had Alzheimer's disease, came to live with me. I was an only child, and therefore responsibility fell to me entirely. One of my daughters had an ugly divorce and she moved in with her two boys. It was a difficult time for a number of years, and time stopped for me—including my writing.

Meanwhile, the editor who bought *Shadow Bear* left Doubleday. Editors regularly change companies and I lost my editor. When I changed genres at first, no one in the field of young adult books knew my work. So it was like starting out all over again.

*You teach students. You have seen them coming into their voice or falsetto.*
Yes, it's interesting. I taught a course, "Playing the Writing Game," which taught teachers how to teach children to write, to produce their own books. That was a wonderful experience.

Then the language-arts coordinator called me to report that the children who took the course and were now in high school were tested and received the highest marks for creative writing. He said they could zero in directly to the school where my writing course was used.

What I tried to do with those young children was to show them that their voices were valuable. Their voices were important. This was completely opposite what I was given in school.

*Could you identify potential writers in these young children?*
Yes. They were imaginative and creative. The most creative people are not the most productive because they may not have that drive to produce. They are not builders.

Talent is one thing, and the drive to express it is another. Someone may have talent and great ideas, but give up or not work on it. Someone else may not have as much talent, but work at it more and perfect it. The drive allows one to succeed.

I have about 300 adult students at this time. There is a six-week span while they work on their lesson. My students are from all over the world: Japan, Korea, etc. They come to me via the Institute of Children's Literature in Reading Ridge, Connecticut.

*Do you see "voice" change, become clearer, more authentic, during this teaching process?*
Their first assignment is to choose a picture and write a story about it. Many of them do not understand viewpoint and I try to make this clear to them. I see the characters develop.

I see some writing in an encyclopedic way. I tell them learning should be fun.

Some struggle with nonfiction. They turn to fiction and I see the talent they have for expressing themselves. Some can write both nonfiction and fiction well. But I find some lean one way or the other.

*Your answer to the question about your nemesis for you is: obsession. Can you say more about your nemesis?*
Just this week I hit this point in the middle of a book. "The muddle in the middle." You can go in different directions. I did a whole chapter yesterday, and thought about it overnight. This morning, I decided it was leading me to a different road. And I am going to rewrite it before my 3 o'clock class. This is the first draft of a story about a kidnapping. I had also thought I'd add a subplot of someone with bulimia.

But if you get to a sluggish point, you've lost the audience. You want to keep a pace. It's similar to a ballgame or a dance.

*Is another story pulling at you to be told?*
That may be what it is; it takes me to a different pathway. I do not write with an outline, as do some people who know exactly where they are going. This story started from a magazine story about a child with a snow globe. Similar to the story of Dr. Chen, this has evolved into a much longer story.

The child relates to the snow globe as if she is in the snow globe. Her family is divorced and she remembers herself in New Hampshire. I use that imagery, as she sees herself as if she is in a snow globe.

There is a handicapped boy of about 16 years in the story, who helps the girl. At the end she has the handicapped boy's hand and she is dancing. She is in the Boston Public Gardens, and petals from the magnolia blossoms are floating around them—similar to the snow in the snow globe.

*Talking about obsession. You mentioned being able to let go of the story. Is obsession the story holding onto you or you holding onto the story?*
It would be me holding onto the story. It's focusing onto it like a child might. "Where is it?" "Is it on someone's desk?" I very much want it to be seen. If I could just talk to the editor and convince him/her to read it. It can be just plain luck—being with the right editor at the right time when someone picks it up and reads it and likes it.

I know it is very competitive. And I know the desks are piled high. It is as if magic is involved.

# Carolivia Herron

*Looking out at multiplicity, and choosing*

### GENRE
Epic; praise-song; early childhood; academic

### PUBLICATIONS INCLUDE
*Nappy Hair*
*Thereafter Johnnie*
*Selected Works of Angelina Weld Grimke* (editor)

*How would you describe your writing voice?*
I have many voices. My main writing voice is one that deals with human voices; it weaves them together, rather than a single voice. I'm recovering from multiple-personality disorder, so this is not just something I'm making up as a technique, but as a way my mind has worked for much of my life, and if you look at many of my writings, you'll find that there is a single voice.

Just as in multiple-personality disorder, there is a strong major personality that pulls the other ones together. The others are in conversation with each other, and the major voice actually tends to look down on them from a height. Not "look down" as in "belittle." Looks over, hears them, and then speaks them out, almost into a space, in a certain way.

It is very clear. I can see all of this. I see the main voice as Jane and she looks over all the other voices that are in conversation. Then Jane chooses from their conversation the artistic—the sculpted, artistic, literary conversation—which she then repeats. I actually do not have that any more; it's been years since all the personalities came together. But I still sustain the technique as a part of myself. It is a way I've learned to think and work.

*You named Jane as the synthesizer?*
Jane is the artistic voice or the integrating voice, actually is not the synthesizer. Essentially I had three personalities, each of which had two names, two different parts: one name that was actually one of my names, and another name that came out of various experiences.

Jane is the counterpart of Carolivia, Carolivia of course, being my name, as I am now. There's Carol and Anna-Marie, a pair. There's Carol Olivia, and Peter (Peter is the only male persona). And Carolivia and Jane.

They have three different tasks, usually. I think of myself as—it's very hard for me now, because I'm so unified now, that I have to actually think. There was a time when it came so fast, and I could just tell you what they were.

But the scholar, novelist, teacher Peter is the academician: I got my Ph.D. as Carol Olivia Herron, and the counterpart is Peter. When I was teaching at Harvard and Mount Holyoke, Peter was in the ascendancy.

Jane has always been the writer. Carolivia at first started out as just a thing in which all the others conversed, and then slowly began choosing from all the various ones: "What is me? What is myself?" And then became one from that—the synthesizer, the one that's unifying.

We'll be getting into *Nappy Hair* I'm sure in our talk. *Nappy Hair* is oral poetry, just as many of the old epics are. My study is of epic literature, and that concept of epic fits in to this Anna-Marie.

I had a terrible history of abuse. It did not come from my parents; it came from people outside the home. My parents were unaware of it.

One reason why I recovered so well is that in my home it was wonderful. I had no problem in my home itself.

The visual part of my work, the visions are all from the Anna-Marie part. I'm right-handed, but if you noticed when I was on the computer I'm using my left hand. Anna-Marie is left-handed, and the visual part is left-handed, so that the mouse is left-handed, because it is dealing with the visual interface on the computer. When I write, it is only right-handed. So it is a complicated kind of thing.

*One question I wrote down is that you have so many vectors in your writing and in your interests—what is the hub? Your academic interests vector off in seemingly diverse, disparate directions, yet they somehow come together in you.*

Yes, I think of it as actually quite unified, perhaps more unified than most people, if you will. Because if you look at it, at every interest, the epic is what I'm after. I love epic.

Every morning I walk by the ocean and meditate. I feel quite often that when I meditate I look down over the whole universe. I look over many universes, and look down on the earth and all its things going on, and make decisions about it and the way I want to be and how to go. And about the past, from going to school to learn about epics, in an official kind of way, to writing novels and oral poetry, to every other aspect.

I think you would see the interest in creating an oral story for my group, my group being many particular groups.

I am African-American, I am Jewish, which is not particularly well-known, and I am of course a woman. I am a U.S. American. And all those sorts of things come together in my wanting to tell the story about epic.

I also want to gather the story about epic, which is why I run down to Washington every other week with these fifth-graders. I want to get them into telling their epic story. I think the story is there, and that I want to create, indeed I am creating, using *Nappy Hair* and some other children's stories (if you want to call them that), fairy tales, as a framework to call forth and develop the song of a people—where their songs will intersect with my songs and perhaps take over my song.

And it's almost as if I used call-and-response for the first time overtly in this text, but that's what I'm doing.

*I enjoyed reading* Nappy Hair. *The listener is verbal, has a voice, and there is the affirmation of the listener even as you're reading it. It is so much fun to read.*
Yes, exactly. That is why it had to be this way.

*Did you come up with the technique of the different-sized types?*
No, that was Random House. They knew what I was after. They understood it—rather well, I must say.

*And when you were writing it was stereophonic?*
Oh, yes, absolutely. Indeed all my writing has been. But nothing more so than this. This one demands it. This is a story that cannot even go forward unless there is an answer. If the audience did not answer, the story would stop, unlike other work where you could come out and carry forth.

I was showing it to the students in this fifth grade, and said, "You could tell this story in Standard English, for example"—and I did. They enjoyed it, and I said, [speaking in plain monotones] "My Uncle Mordecai told this story at the backyard picnic, Uncle Mordecai told it," and so forth, "Brenda, don't you have some nappy hair on your head? Well, it's your hair."

This [style] doesn't need a response. It doesn't need somebody to say "Well, yup, don't you know!"—doesn't need it, if you do it in the standard formal English.

*You can read it with a British accent, but it feels very freeze-dried . . .*
Yes! The kids all cracked up. This story demands response in order to go forward. And it's a choice I made in this tale.

Now one of the things about this story is that it's not a story. You may have noticed that. There is really not a plot to it. There are little sections that are plot-like and depend on what came before, but it is a praise song, an African praise song set in African-American context.

And a praise song just picks something and praises it. And a praise song does not have to have a beginning, middle, and end, you see?

Some of the critics have not understood this, and most of the reviews have been good. I do not mind a bad review, if it finds something really there. But it really is frustrating when they say, "Well, where is the plot?" As if I didn't know that it has no plot! You know, it's just really frustrating: of course there's no plot.

*I interviewed Phyllis Hoge, a Quaker poet, and I asked her how her poetry connects with her spirituality. She said: "Praise! Praise! Everything is praise." Even her dark or painful poetry, to her, is praise for being alive. For just being. Your praise song is very affirming of life, and of connection.*
It is. And the context of the praise singer, in the African communities— what do you actually do to keep the kings and the nobles in line? If people are being praised, and to make sure [they stay in line], "You wouldn't do such-and-such, would you? Because you are so wonderful! Therefore you would not hurt the this-one and the that-one and the other." It is a way of controlling when there isn't any real power to control but there is verbal power and cultural power to help make the people who are high and praiseworthy *be* praiseworthy, be heroic, and of course that's one of the things I'm after.

I delight in my hair. Many people, unfortunately, have not delighted in nappy hair. So I have had very interesting responses in communities where "nappy hair" was almost considered an insult. When I was growing up perhaps it was considered so [i.e., insulting]. Not so much, now, but when I go into a black classroom and I say, "I am going to read you my book entitled *Nappy Hair*," I usually get these gasps of horror. Like [gasp] "*How* could you say such a thing?"

Then finally, they listen and they listen and they finally get it. The kids get it fast. Sometimes the grown-ups don't get it as fast, but the kids get it.

*"Nappy" can be disparaging? I didn't know the word.*
It is an insult, yes indeed. And it is a word that many many white people do not know at all. There is no black person who does not know it.

From the time you are little you are a nappy-headed kid, you are a nappy-headed chile, "Why don't you go in the house and comb your hair?! And smooth it out or whatever you can." I actually do have the nappiest hair in my immediate family. I don't know that I have the nappiest hair in the *world*, but [laughs] the story is about me.

It is the story my Uncle Richard told about me. My mother has added a few lines and my brother a few lines, and I gathered parts of it from all the family. I wove it together into a tale, into a praise song, but it is based on real things that happened.

*What is your earliest memory of writing?*
My earliest memory is about three years old, when I wrote my first poem. My mother read the *Child's Garden of Verses* to me over and over again. I fell in love with the *Child's Garden of Verses,* and I wrote a poem. I didn't know how to write yet, until the following year, so I had to keep it in my head for a year—oral poetry, right? [Laughs]

I tried to write it, a very silly little thing, of course, a four-year-old poem, but I still think of it as significant, in spite of its simplicity. I thought about it deeply, and made a choice of the words which had a lot of hidden meaning for me, even though it didn't convey it in the main meaning. I'll tell you the poem, if you'd like to hear it. It is:

> *The rain is raining on the trees*
> *It falls on the ground,*
> *and it falls on me.*

Now that's the poem, all of it. What I still think, in spite of my 50 years now, as an important moment of the poem, is: I wanted a poem in which the rain fell on successively lower things, with me being the lowest.

In my imagination, the ground was the lowest thing, so the first writing of it, the rain is falling on the tree and falls on the grass, and it falls on me. And then changing it, it falls on the ground—the change between grass and ground took weeks of decision-making. I still don't know which one is right, but I think my final version was:

*Tree, grass, ground,*

with me as the lowest level. And that was an expression of my melancholy.

I did not recall my memories until [several] years ago. But they had already started through the abuse I had seen and endured, including the murder of my baby brother. That poem was related directly to the death of my brother. It was an important moment.

I prayed every night from the time I was 4 till I was 11, that I would grow up and write the book. "If I can't write, Lord, just take me on out of here, I've had enough." It was so strong, it was the most passionate prayer. Every night.

I stopped [this prayer] when I read *Paradise Lost,* by Milton, of course, because—that wasn't the sign that I was a writer, and yet it was. Somehow when I read *Paradise Lost,* the very title reminded me of my brother.

It was like, when my brother died, I had this wonderful house, home, my parents, I was a first child. . . . I was walking down the street, my grandmother took me away from him, and—holding my hand, walking down the street, she had tears just coming down that face, because there's a sudden death, of course. My mother was taken out screaming, and my grandmother was walking down the street, with these tears coming down her face. I can remember looking up at her face, and saying, "I knew it, I knew it all the time, I knew those smiles weren't the real thing. I knew it."

He died in 1950, I was born in 1947. Three years, a little over three years old.

I knew that Paradise had been lost. So when I saw the title of that book, I knew, I have to read this book.

*You read it when you were 11?*
When I was 11. I knew that I had found something that was my promise. It was the epic, of course.

Now, if I think about a child who prays from the time of 3 to 11 to write a book, you *know* that child's going to write a book. You don't have to worry about it.

But when you're *in* it, you don't know that. I think of it now, I think how funny that I would be so concerned that it [writing a book] may not have happened. But you can't...

*It was keeping some truth of you alive. And a promise that more of you would be known...*
Yes. I was buying these new shoes, and somebody asked me, because I used my Harvard card to get a discount, and they said, "What's your favorite book?"

And I said to myself, "May my tongue cling to the roof of my mouth if I ever say it's not *Paradise Lost* by John Milton." I said that to myself. I didn't go into all this, but "May my right hand forget its cunning!" And I just said, *"Paradise Lost."*

They freaked, of course, how could anybody say that? But even in a situation where it would not be politic to say that, to admit to it, I could never deny what that book did. It took me out of Hell. When I was 11 years old. And carried me.

*So you began writing more when you were 11?*
I wrote a lot of poetry, through 11, and pretty much stopped when I was 11. And read more, for a while. It was, perhaps a frantic kind of "I have to write or I may never write" at first, so—

*So you wrote from 4 until 11?*
Well, 4, no. I would say more 5 to 11. I wrote that one poem, and then maybe when I was 5 years old I started to write more. And I still wrote some poetry between 11 and 17, 18. I published my first small collection of poetry at 17 or 18. And I wrote poetry until I was 25 or so, then started writing fiction.

I switched to fiction. It became my career. I am so abstract, mythical and poetic in my writing, that if I write poetry, nobody knows who I am, I'm just too far out. I almost need plot, or a hint of plot, or something to pull it into the world people see. And I think it's good for me. Another person may need to go off wherever that is, but I like bringing it to the stuff of this world.

*Bringing it into this dimension, of others.*
Yes. That's the reason why I talk about the visions I can see. To me it is like this table, but since other people can't see it, it is hard to convey what I've imagined. With the power of the computer, I can convey it, along with the words, even though my drawings are not anything . . . [laughs] like William Blake's, say.

*How have you had to defend your writing voice?*
When my multiple personalities first came out, my psychoanalyst asked me, or asked Anna-Marie, "Are any more of you in there?" And she said "There are a few more that are nearby. We can be hundreds and thousands, but those are the characters of the stories." That's what she said, that was the answer. See, those are the stories.

I yearn for what Toni Morrison talks about, her distance from her characters. I have nothing like that. I cannot get there. To try to get there would be to deny my own way of feeling and knowing. It is a strange feeling, when I began to learn how to be a fiction writer, to know that everybody is me, there's no character in my books who isn't me.

I keep talking about one day, I'll write a character who isn't me. That is the dream of my creative life. [Laughs]

*How has your writing voice changed over time? You already answered how you pick your genre—it picked you, and continues to pick you.*
Oh yes, I do not see any of them [the stories] diverging from the epic.

My novel *Asenath* is an epic in which a graduate student at the University of Pennsylvania cannot get her dissertation done; she keeps falling into her books and ending up in various ancient epics. She is writing her dissertation on epics.

In one of the exercises in epic studies, she translates some material from ancient Egyptian and from ancient Greek, finds that it is the same material, and that what it is saying is that the person with the nappiest hair in any particular place is the queen. And then she goes on to realize that this book is about herself (she has nappy hair, of course). She describes how her uncle talks about her having her nappy hair.

So *Nappy Hair* is extracted from that epic. It is so delightful to so many people that I read it to.

African epic has a very interesting history. There was a woman, I think Ruth Finnegan is her name, and she's probably in total embarrassment at having stated in the year 1969 (she's at Oxford, I think) that there was no such thing as an African epic.

This was a wonderful, horrible thing to say, of course, because it outraged so many people that they all raced to Africa, determined to find an epic.

My own professor at Penn was among these, who felt, "What do you mean, there's no epic?" He went to this famous African poet, and told the poet to tell the story he sings; it takes about six minutes to sing. Then he asked the poet if he could sing it any longer. And the poet sang it for 15 minutes. "Can you sing it longer than that?" He sang it for half an hour. "Can you sing it any longer than that?" He sang it for an hour. "Can you sing it longer than that?" He sang it for two hours.

The professor said, "How long could you sing it if you sang it as long as you wanted, as you could?" The poet said, "Oh, when I'm back at home, I sing it for three weeks, like for four hours every evening!"

So, he was singing an epic that could take up five or six times the size of the *Iliad*. Nobody had ever asked him! Everybody had gone there recording these things, and said, "I've got ten minutes. Sing me a song." Well, what do you expect? They hadn't understood how long the epic is.

The same thing with *Nappy Hair*. This book could be as long as the *Iliad* by the time I get finished with it, bringing in the stories. For example, if in the middle of telling *Nappy Hair*, when he says, "And then the angels walk up to God," what if somebody, instead of saying "What?" had said, "You ain't seen no angels!" He'd have gone on for 15 minutes. "Who ain't seen no angels? I been seeing angels! I saw the angel just the other day, he was . . . and then last week! Who—what are you talking?" Can't you see how it would go on and on and on? And the story would be longer and longer and longer.

I'm not saying that I'm writing an African epic, of course. I'm not in that culture specifically, but what I'm thinking of—when I talk about putting this onto a computer or onto some hypertext system, you could start seeing all the places it can go. We're talking about a very long work. And then you'll see that it's an epic. I believe that you could have a *Nappy Hair* epic.

*You mean something that many people could add to?*
Yes. I feel that this is what is bringing me to the next century. I disagree with our concept that somehow a work has to be by one person in order to be very good. I think that it is possible to have an epic work of the quality of the *Iliad*, of *Paradise Lost*, of Thomas Mann, of all those people who wrote great works or great series of works, with a single unifying voice or self. They have influenced us to think that's the only way [great works] can be.

And of course we say it about Homer, because we don't know whether that's a single unifying person.

I suspect that there has to be some kind of unifying frame, or subject. In true call-and-response, of a story—if you think that this would be the same story without the responses, then okay, but if you think that these kids would add anything, what's supposed to say that even a longer intrusion by somebody else would not be a good part?

I have the capacity to set up a frame, a voice frame, or a concept, a way of looking at a thing, and then start calling forth: "Now I'll be the caller and you respond to me," and doing it in such a way that pretty soon the responses get longer and longer.

And maybe a whole book, a chapter, a whole something, is by the fifth-grade class at Katie C. Lewis Elementary School in Washington, D.C., and maybe the next one will be by the Roxbury School, with second-graders.

And why not? I think the 21st century needs that epic—we need to open up the next century with the concept that it is possible not to lose artistic value even when you have many voices. After all, with my many voices—you see why I had to do it! [Laughs] it's personal! [Laughs] Because I've often thought that perhaps I could never be a good writer, if we have so many voices.

*You have the gift to be able to speak with many voices. It is likely, then, that you can listen with many voices, and you can orchestrate many voices, from within or without.*
I hope so, that's what I want. At least, that's what I'm using. And I, indeed, I don't have the multiple personalities any longer, but I have not forgotten what they taught me.

So it is using what I learned, in a way that's more palpable, perhaps, than someone who's trying to imagine the voice of that person over there.

*There are spiritual leaders that claim that our belief in separate existence as individuals to begin with is not true, that there is a one-ness. As one of us grows, it affects everyone.*
Certainly, that's from my philosophy.

*To build a community in the way that you're talking about is to bring a different kind of voice from the "me" generations of the '60s and '70s to the "us" across a number of cultures, barriers, governments . . . the place to do it is the Web. [Laughs]*
Yes. And Anasazi—yes, I think of Anasazi, a West African spider weaving the web.

Anasazi is the name of my multimedia project. I use that image a lot.

*How have you had to defend your voice, and voices?*
Well, it was very hard. It took me 17 years to get *Thereafter Johnnie* published, my first book. It was finished in about 6 years. And then the paperback came out. There are two American editions, and the hardback is out back in Britain.

It took 17 years to get published, not to write. Because my first publisher said that, among other things, "Black people don't write like that. It was very beautiful writing, but it doesn't use black dialect, African-American dialect, at all."

They really had a problem with it. It was tough to sell to people, "It's too mystical—for black people, you know" I'm serious! These are the kinds of things—you want to know how I defend my voice?

I have an article that I wrote, "Social Control on the Arts: Black Women's Writing on Trial." It is a racial piece from a conference held at the Center for Literary and Cultural Studies.

*So you've had to defend not only being a woman but being black, and writing in your style?*
And writing differently—uniquely—from what was considered "right."

*For . . . ?*
For black women. Fortunately for us, we've had Gloria Naylor, Toni Morrison, Alice Walker. Those are women that I most admire, extremely, who carved a path, taught us the way.

People ask me do I mind being called a "black writer." Some people just say, "I'm a writer, don't call me black, don't call me woman."

I like all the adjectives you can put on me.

Because I want it to be that when you hear that somebody is a black woman writer, technologist writer, you say, "Oh wow, it's got to be good." That's what I want people to say.

You know, if you hear somebody is a Russian novelist, don't you say: "Wow, he's got to be good"? You know, Dostoyevsky, Tolstoy? Yet somebody says, "black novelist," they get upset. I don't get it, myself. They say, "I'm a writer, I'm not a 'black writer.'" Well, I am a black woman, Jewish, religious, technological-freak writer. I like all the words. I like all of them.

*That was one of my questions. How much of your identity is writer?*
Somebody asked me how much—about the Jewish-black connection—how much is which? I'm one-hundred percent all of them. It's not divided—divisible.

*So in the dimensions you work in, you're totally writer, and totally everything else?*
Yes. I want all of it—all of it, I want. It's part of the personalities coming together. I can no longer work in a position in which you take my intellect on epics and use only that, or my intellect on black America and use only that.

*What's the role of silence in your voice?*
Everything I publish is read aloud many, many, many times. So many times, it is embarrassing to say. I start at the beginning of a paragraph, and I read one sentence, and I wait. I look up and I wait to see what word comes next in my head. And if the word that comes next in my head is not the one that I have written, then I work it over again, until the silence fills automatically with the next word. And then I do that and then I read two sentences—

I will do that over and over again until I get one paragraph. And then I do the next paragraph, and then I read two paragraphs, and then on and on like that, in any one paragraph. And I walk. I like to have places where I can walk around in a circle. The beach is good for it. And it takes hours and hours. That's the kind of silence and the actual process of writing.

Meditation is another kind of silence; that's a silence of choosing what path to take with the writing, or with anything I do. I meditate in the mornings, by the beach. Of course, that's not filled with silence because the waves are coming in. It is a silence in me as I walk up and down and try to decide.

It is always a case of looking out at multiplicity and choosing one: one path, one string, one thread, one place to go; that is another kind of silence.

*What has been your brick wall, your nemesis in writing?*
I'm never without words. "Hyper-glossia" is the word they have for it. There's never a "what do I write next or how would I ever do it?" I have 20 different ways of doing it, or 50 different ways of doing it.

There are times when I'm writing along it seems to me that it is so good that it can't be me writing. But there is never a sense of barrier. I don't know that I've had that, in the actual writing of fiction, although I do understand you. My hope is that I could get that, by the way.

It is a concept that Yeats had, and he probably had it from somebody else, but his concept was that every writer has what he calls an *automatism*, something you do so well that you'll not even think about it. It just flows out of you, and maybe it is characterization, maybe it is conversation. Maybe it is description.

Mine, if I may say so, is description. Give me something as dull as a black pen on a brown table, and I could write three hundred pages. If I could write most of it badly and only a little bit of it really well, that would be fine. You could drop the bad part and keep the good—the problem is, you can do that, and make all of it pretty good, and none of it really good!

My task is to slow down the writing, stop it, cut it off, find a wall, find a brick, find a writer's block, which I have never known, of any kind. And then, when you take up the pen again, maybe you will get it right. To have the capacity to do descriptions almost always relatively well, is not good enough. You have to do the best that you can do, in order to gain the glue that holds your work together.

*Is there anything else you want to say on voice or writing?*
Yes there is one thing, especially since you're asking about *Nappy Hair*. I'd like to say something about earliest impressions of African-American writings. I started with *A Child's Garden of Verses*, I talked about Milton, but I didn't tell you, my father had two wonderful books of African-American poetry, which he had as a child. I read them, and at first never really did much with them. I loved them, one was a Paul Lawrence Dunbar book, the 19th-century African-American poet, and the other was a collection.

I didn't speak black dialect at all. It was always standard English in the home. My mother decided that it was time for me to have more connection with my peers and groups and so forth, and she taught me to speak one of the Paul Lawrence Dunbar dialect poems, which was a joy. The name of the poem is "In the Morning."

I went to school, in the fifth grade, and recited this poem to the class and to the teacher and all. It was my first moment of performance with the first real sense of having done something real and having the adulation of a crowd. The kids in the class thought it was wonderful, and the teacher thought it was so good. I just never had that before.

I began to become very much involved in reading 19th-century African-American poetry. The tension between the black dialect and the Standard English became a very intriguing connection for me, which comes out in my writing.

If you saw my book *Asenath* that *Nappy Hair* is taken from, this is the only part in African-American dialect, in black dialect, in the whole book. It is a book of Standard English, but this crucial central moment *has* to go into the African-American speech patterns.

I just wanted to share that. To me that was the beginning. I think when I saw the reaction of that group, maybe that became the completion of a heartbeat. You know, you talk about the heartbeat, you hear in your gut, you know that [heartbeat sound], the heartbeat of a different language. It was a part of my life. I think *Nappy Hair* began the day I recited Dunbar in the fifth grade.

*And now you're teaching fifth grade.*
Yes, I was thinking of that. I recited it for them, the Dunbar poem, the other day. They enjoyed that.

# Jill Hackett

*Not writing alone*

**GENRE**

Nonfiction; technical and business writing

*I'm thinking kind of in terms of your own story of voice. What brought you to this study? Why are you doing this study now at this point in your life?* When I first started technical writing, I was more excited about that job than anything I'd ever done, because I really love writing. And now I feel like Alice in Wonderland at the top of a place that's too small for her. I've grown fully into the skills technical writing can give me. The challenges now from technical writing are from the technology, not from the craft.

So I wanted to find a new place, a new way, to use the skills of writing. Technical writing has been a way of backing into writing. I had studied a lot of psychology; I now realize that some of that is because I love the stories in it, and learning more about human character. I love to research, and then turn around and share it, give it out, for someone

---

This interview is conducted by Roni Natov, who was the author's doctoral adviser at Union Institute & University.

else to discover and find. Some of it is that I like to figure out how things work: computers and people.

*Did you always like to write, when you were a child?*
My father and mother gave me a printing press one year for Christmas when I was about eight. It had little rubber type, and I spent a whole week making newspapers, because my father was a newspaperman and I loved his machines, and the printer's ink.

When I was very young, Dad would come home from the paper at 5:30 and wash my hands in his. He'd take my little hands into his big rough inked-up hands and with the scratchy Lava soap, we'd wash our hands together.

So before the age of five, every night, I had printer's ink rubbed into me. I still love the smell of printer's ink in a print shop. The excitement of and the connection to writing being a way of giving voice to community, because my dad was editor of a small-town newspaper. Writing was always a way of connecting to others in a way that was exciting, and affirming to the other people as well. Giving them more voice. More visibility.

There are other pieces of my self as a child that I didn't understand was about writing until I interviewed these women authors. For instance, when I first went to kindergarten I drew pictures of people with huge, huge ears—their ears the size of elephants'—because I loved listening to people.

Rachel Vail talks about how she thought her gift was eavesdropping, because she could listen to several conversations at once and remember them. And the place to use this gift was as a spy, so when she went to college she decided to go to Georgetown because what better place to be a spy than Washington, D.C. Rachel uses this gift now in listening to her characters' voices for her novels.

I knew that I loved listening to people, and it was only because my kindergarten teacher, who was my mother, said, "You have to get the ears in proportion" that I put the ears back where they belonged.

I guess I was gathering material from a very young age about people, and that was what psychology was, but it is not my passion the way writing is my passion.

*What do you think writing does for the self that psychology doesn't do for you?*
In psychology, when you listen to another person's story, it flows through you, but when you give it back to them, you are supposed to, or historically have been supposed to, distill yourself back out of it. So that you can be as clear a mirror as possible. Making no ripples, so they see only themselves. Psychology is shifting now so that the therapist can bring more of their self into the therapuetic relationship—you can have the therapeutic dyad which includes a human being as a therapist. This is new. But writing has always been that way.

A course I took on history of psychology posited that psychology really came out of religion. Both seek to create a fullness of life, the good life, for the participant. Both religion and psychology use the therapeutic communication, the confession.

Writing is that same kind of trust and interaction pouring into one another. In a good piece of writing, the reader can invest and receive, so there's more of a communion, a commune-ication in writing, than there is in psychology.

*And speaking of seeing yourself as a writer at five, or real little, can you think of your own life in terms of turning points as a writer, when your own voice developed or shifted or became many voices at different points in your life?*
There were times when my voice would become very clear and it would scare me, so I would go back into my shell and not speak for awhile. Because it surprised me, the sound that came out of me. And I wasn't supposed to make that sound somehow.

When I took a self-defense class, the first thing we were taught was to stomp our feet and yell real loud "No," and "911." One of the girls, a very young twenty-something, burst into tears. The instructor went over and said, "What? what's up with this?" The girl said, "I've never yelled 'No' before, and it felt so good."

There were times when I would write something, that it would seem so clear, or so loud, or something, that, like the groundhog, I would go in until later. I guess there is something about turning 50, there's not going to be a later, so it's now! [Laughs] I'm not as afraid to let that voice come out and squawk, and make loud screechy sounds until I get it. Until I learn my song.

*Can you give me an example of a couple of times?*
Sure. Two times come to mind. One was in high school. I was in a writing class with a teacher that I respected very much, J. B. Deihl. I wrote a piece that came from my gut. It was very personal to me. Mr. Deihl began to read this piece in class and I just couldn't look up. I was overcome with emotion because I felt so vulnerable in this piece. No one in the class knew who it was, Mr. Deihl hadn't said who wrote it. We were having a discussion on whether there was male or female voice in writing, and Mr. Deihl wanted people to guess whether this was a girl or a boy writing.

*Did they?*
No. He stopped. He ended up stopping because he looked at me and saw how emotional I was, that he stopped reading the piece. I wish he'd gone forward in that moment. I wish I had been able to ask him to.

The second turning point was in English 101 Freshman year. We had to write a piece on Henry James' *The Ambassadors*. I had been working and working and working on my pieces of writing, rewriting them two and three times, really going over the words. As I look back I probably was taking the voice out of it, much like Megan was taught to "erase herself," and polish it until there was no person.

I really didn't like *The Ambassadors*, and was unable to make myself finish this book. So I kept asking for extensions on the critique. When I got my third and final extension, I did the sacrilegious act of sitting down at my electric Smith Corona typewriter and knocking off a satire of this awful (to me) book. I didn't care what the assignment was; I couldn't write a critique. I was imitating James' voice, kind of acting his voice in my writing, and, I thought, mocking it.

But the professor, who loved James, thought I did a terrific job, and the first thing, the very next class, read it to the class, prefacing her reading with, "This is what happens when absolutely every word is worked over and chosen carefully." I hadn't done that in this piece, I had ripped it off, first draft. I had worked on all the other pieces I wrote for her.

I made a decision then to go underground again with my writing. It was too important to me personally to expose myself to a process of teaching that I felt didn't fit my way of learning. With 20-20 hindsight, I see that actually with all the extensions I got on that piece, I probably was writing it, just not with pen in hand. It was, as Jean Shinoda Bolen writes, "perking on one of my cauldrons."

It was bubbling in my unconscious or preconscious. And it wasn't what the professor specifically asked for, but it was my full response to the question. She asked for a critique, and my response was this satire.

*Very interesting. So you felt, first of all, totally misunderstood.*
Yes. I didn't understand how they were commenting on my voice. They in fact were hearing me. I wasn't hearing me in the way that they were hearing.

*Or what they were hearing is a little far from what you thought you were saying. Can you describe your writing voices, or is there a host, a main voice? You've talked about the technical writer, but what are some of the other voices and how have they developed over the years?*
My main writing voice is this logical, mathematical rational mechanical voice that I have trained through technical writing. Allowing any other range of voice now has been difficult until I found a way to use that technical voice in service of the others. I give that skill set the task of organization and craft, dealing with the authoring tools and technology and indexing.

I think in pictures, the way Carolivia thinks in pictures first. I "see" or sense an image on an inner screen. I didn't think that was the way you were supposed to think, until I learned about intelligence testing. Some people think first in pictures, and then put words to them. Some people first get words, and hear words. Other people get ticker-tape thoughts, that don't really have a voice sound, they just are knowings that come out. Other people will get a kinetic hit on something and then begin to write with that.

My primary muted voice that I have not used much in writing is the visual (although I've used it in creating graphics for technical manuals). I like metaphor and love to play with the sounds of words, and rhythms of words—that's the musician in me. So I guess I want to sing and dance in writing, but I've only been able to do documentary. [Laughs] There's musical comedy in me yet.

*When we were talking yesterday, you mentioned the word sanctuary, and this feels like a sanctuary for you, this circle of women?*
Yes. Here are a number of published authors and really interesting human beings, who have come to their process in very different ways. This helps me speak back to the educational authorities, and the personal authorities in my life who have told me at times I was doing it wrong. It allows me to figure out what is my process, and allow my process to be evolving —not "you figure it out once," but that it's going to shift and change as I change.

*I was going to ask you, being so close to these other women, what have they done for you? But you've answered that.*
I have their pictures all around me as I'm writing.

*Literally?*
Literally. I got that idea from Gina Barreca's office, which has layers of notes, cartoons, memorabilia. It is like this paper cocoon. I am usually a neatnik when I write, and that's what my technical writer needs: clear horizontal spaces, no visual distractions. Clear the decks. Now my window has Yoko and her sister Ko, and everyone's pictures here, with notes from some of them. It's plastered all over. I draw them up around me as I write, like a comforter.

*Fantastic.*
So I'm not writing alone.

*So you're not writing alone. Jill, I think there are key things that you've talked about, and I just want to touch on them, reflect them back to you. You mentioned sanctuary, educational and personal authority, those are interesting terms to reflect on.*

*I was talking to a friend of mine yesterday, we went to the Y and we were talking—we both teach at Brooklyn College, in the English department. We both came to feel that as teachers, the way we've grown is to give permission, allow more space for students to discover their own voice. And also, the other ingredient is to inspire. So inspiration and permission. That's basically what I think students need. And some guidance.*

*Another thing you might want to talk about is their struggles. It doesn't sound like anybody just drifted into voice and that was it. There were struggles along the way.*

Megan used the term "creative wound." There's something about getting wounded that brings out either resiliency, that deep anger—and you either fold or you grow and strengthen from it. And your voice gets clarified by the scarring.

*Of course many fold. It doesn't seem like wounding is necessary, it's just part of our culture.*

And some of us fold, and then when we're 50, then we try again!

*That's not even folding. That's growing. But see, one of the things I wanted you to think about is how you grow. How you've been growing. It's not like at 50 this happened.*

There's something that I call "cheats and stalls." Stalls are creative procrastinations. Cheats cheat out the part that's afraid, so I can write anyway, and that's what technical writing has been for me.

My father-in-law learned to walk as a toddler by carrying a 78 rpm record around. He could cruise and hold on to things, but he didn't think he could walk across the room. So his mother gave him a phonograph record. And as long as he had a record in his hand he could walk anywhere. When he fell down and it broke, he couldn't get up. So she'd give him another record, and he would stand up, and he'd walk.

There are ways that in our writing, we do that. We say, "Oh well, we can write essays, or we can write a poem," but really finding the fullness of voice—one day we just get up and walk.

There are so many ways to use this material. Every time I go in some direction, I'm using the tuning fork of "Is this really about voice?" There are lots of stories in here about process also. Which informs voice, but what I'm trying to do is define and describe the attributes and elements of voice in writing. Then some things need to be put aside and not spoken of even though they're in the material.

*I think that's a good idea. Like, what will you illuminate out of all the stories that are in your head. I want you to think about what you want to pass on to your readers.*

It's a very different process than technical writing, where you can force it. Writing with your true voice has its own strange time. Every morning I wake up with a new piece getting clearer. And I can't make it happen, I have to let it happen. I have to listen for it. I have to allow the unfolding in its own wisdom and time.

# Louise M. Wisechild

*The "I must write" voice*

### GENRE
Memoirs; political commentary

### PUBLICATIONS INCLUDE
*The Mother I Carry: A Memoir of Healing from Emotional Abuse*
*The Obsidian Mirror: An Adult Healing from Incest*
*She Who Was Lost Is Remembered: Healing from Incest Through Creativity* (editor)

*Tell me about defending your voice, the lock and key of your diary.*
When I wrote *The Obsidian Mirror*, I was in a writers' group, which met every week, with a teacher, and I never took my book there. I was getting good writing practice in the group. I had a group of friends who were also writing, which was invaluable, but I didn't take *The Obsidian Mirror* anywhere until the first major draft was done. Then I started to have people read it.

    This was really one of the best decisions I made, because the book was so close to me. And there was so little information about incest at that time. It is a triggering book; people have a strong reaction to it. I intentionally wrote it so that the reader would accompany me on my journey of remembering and healing from abuse. It raised a lot of childhood issues for people.

In retrospect, it feels like some angel, some bit of inner wisdom, encouraged me to protect my work until I was strong enough to put it out.

I spent five years working on each of my two memoirs. After I'd worked on *The Obsidian Mirror* a couple years, I showed a chapter of it to Barbara Wilson, who was teaching at Flight of the Mind women's writing conference. She was also the co-owner of Seal Press. She said that Seal might be interested in the book when it was done. So three years later I took it there. Naturally I wanted them to jump up and down with joy and pay me lots of money, which was very optimistic, especially for a small press.

I felt, and I still feel this, three books later, that the whole experience of publishing is mysterious. And it is in many ways stacked against the writer. Of everyone in the entire process, the writer is the most poorly paid and the least well informed. And I wanted them to like me, the press, all of which works against the kind of business sense that that part of writing really calls for. Because then the book goes from being your baby to being a product.

That's why now I'm learning about self-publishing for my essays and even for my fiction. I like the idea of having more control over publishing, and technology is now making that possible. I've gotten used to the idea that everyone doesn't have to read my work for it to be successful.

For *The Obsidian Mirror*, it took Seal Press about three and a half months to let me know whether they were going to publish it or not. Incest was a little-known field, so they had different therapists read it. Plus I had chosen a particular technique—using inner voices to tell my story—and they wanted to check that out.

Overall, Seal was supportive of me at the time, but I often felt lost in terms of playing this new role of author. I think this has taken me many years to grow into, this belief in my own voice.

For a long time I felt excruciatingly shy after giving people my books to read or even telling them what I had written. I'd be afraid to see people after they'd read them.

*Because you were so vulnerable in your writing?*
Yes. I was afraid of what people would think of me. It was really self-revealing. And of course, I was still working with my shame—that these terrible things happened to me—as well as with the culture's denial of sexual abuse.

*But you did it anyway. That was stronger than the fear: you would give your writing to people even though you were then afraid to see them—that's interesting.*
Right, right.

I also felt strongly that I wanted people to read the books. Especially as I began to realize that what I had hoped—which is that my book would help people—was happening. I was so lucky in that a lot of people who read my book wrote to me. I felt connected with the outer world and other survivors of childhood abuse for the first time. That experience for me was also really, really powerful.

*Creating a community?*
Yes. And the opportunity to meet amazing people through the teaching and speaking that my books allowed. Writing actually helped me create a world that was different than the one that I thought I was in. Not as different as I *thought* it was, when I went back and reread some of my early writings! [Laughs]

*Qualitatively it must have been different. Allowed who you are today to have survived. Did anyone validate you and say, "You can write?"*
Teachers.

*But that's not when the decision came?*
No. I've never really tried to pinpoint the events that surrounded it, but from early on, I always felt like I had a purpose. That was very confus-

ing to me in my childhood, because I couldn't understand how I would ever get heard. I felt there was something large I was going to do, and yet that wasn't reflected by my family.

  I got more reinforcement in school. People would say, "You have potential." By the time I was ten, I began to realize that the skill of being able to write was very useful in school. And [I realized] that some people couldn't write. At least not . . .

*Not the way you could.*
Or that they didn't like to write or felt they couldn't. In service of whatever messages they had gotten about writing. On the other hand, it never failed to surprise me, all the way through university: that I could write a sentence or a paragraph that actually made sense, was interesting, and which made me successful in that environment.

*Have you ever had to defend your voice?*
One thing that it's taken me years to really integrate is the fact that people's reactions to my work, or to anything for that matter, is about them. This is true even though the writing is about me. I think meditation has helped me see that more clearly in the last couple years. But at first it was very emotional.

  One of the biggest experiences that comes to mind is when the reviewer for a national gay and lesbian newspaper wrote that I was, essentially, crazy, and that the book was too painful to read. She really blew it off, big time. I was outraged. I obsessed painfully about her response.

  But I did notice that when there's a direct attack like that, I rise to defend myself. That experience in itself is validating because it made me look for support. It also made me validate my own work, so that I really knew I wasn't crazy. Then the question was whether I should write her a letter.

  There is supposed to be something noble about not defending yourself as a writer, about not talking back and continuing to clarify after one's words are in print. But I really believe we as writers need to keep communicating—at least I do.

At that time, some other people, who I didn't know and who had read my book, came to my defense pretty strongly in their letters to this publication. So altogether it turned out to be a really positive experience.

*Did you write a letter responding to that editor?*
Yes, I wrote a letter and no, I didn't send it. I'd already heard from Bonnie Arthur, another writer, that she had written defending my work. Just the way karma or whatever it is works, the person who wrote that review actually wanted to interview me a couple years later when the anthology I edited came out. And I said no.

Now, I hope I would engage in a dialogue with the reviewer before making this type of decision, but that's because I've grown in my confidence about communicating and I feel less threatened by challenges.

This is also the result of my more recent political writing and my decision to publish it locally. I live on an island and I have written a series of essays advocating non-violence in response to terrorism. The papers printed some vehement letters in response to mine, some saying I should move to a Communist country and that I was unpatriotic because I was advocating non-violent solutions. I also handed out my essays downtown and put them in shops. It is the most vulnerable I've ever been with my work because I was with my words, in person, in my own small town.

Some stores refused to carry the essays. People I'd always felt easy with started avoiding me. But I determined to treat everyone in a friendly way because we are neighbors. That has helped me learn a lot about communicating with people who disagree with me. But it doesn't mean I will stop talking about peace and non-violence anymore than I'll ever stop talking about child abuse.

The other part has been learning to accept the positive, to really take in the rewards of writing. There's that wonderful glow of having said what I wanted, of feeling pleased that the passion found form. Then there's the positive feedback from others.

I make it a practice, especially when there's a lot of opposition directed at me, to recount the support I've received. I'd rather be touched by the support than enraged by the opposition. And when I do this accounting, I always find more support than criticism.

I keep more distance now between myself and the emotional venom that can be part of someone else's response to my writing. Instead I try to see if there's a challenge in their words that I can address so as to further educate people about the need for peace and sustainability. Mostly now I try to focus on developing my own opinions instead of defending myself.

Right now I think the most effective way to work is locally, but I also know that it takes courage. I feel like my books were a great preparation for this peace work.

Having done these other books, I'm really so aware of how astonishingly fortunate I was, when *The Obsidian Mirror* came out. It came out in that tiny little window when you could actually publish work about abuse, but that [window] closed almost entirely. It is really hard to get that kind of work out now. It has had its little time as a trend.

*It's too risky for the publishers?*
Yes. A lot of political stuff has happened, especially around the False Memory Syndrome. There's an attitude now that people are making up this childhood memory. There's a fear of lawsuits. But basically I think we don't want to look at child abuse the same way we don't want to look at the terrible cost of war. It's been pushed underground so we can keep pretending everything is fine, all evidence to the contrary.

When [*The Obsidian Mirror*] first came out I got incredible reviews. *Publishers Weekly* called it "a singular literary achievement." It was like the universe was smiling on me. And it was.

From experience, now, the most devastating thing is not direct attack, or needing to defend the voice in that way, but being ignored. *The Mother I Carry*, for example, was barely reviewed. Most people who have read *The Obsidian Mirror* don't even know there's a sequel to it. For a long time that was really painful.

*Was it as powerful an experience for you to write the second book as the first?*
It was harder, somehow, the second book. I think it was harder because although speaking about incest at the time that I wrote *The Obsidian Mirror* was taboo, I think that it's true that we don't have very high expectations of fathers in our culture, or of men, from a feminist perspective.

But to write about mothers is crossing a taboo that feminists share. It is so loaded, especially for women. I was at a survivor conference and people were telling me, "Well, I bought *The Mother I Carry* and I haven't read it yet." They bought it two years ago. Just the topic is very frightening.

*I agree, it hits deep archtypes. We have issues here of what is real and feminine, and woman and mother and nurturing. There is a myth in our culture that holds, if a woman gives birth she is automatically nurturing, and good at parenting. It does not necessarily follow.*
Right. We have a myth of family just like we have a myth of ourselves as a nation. It's hard work to take apart those myths so healing can happen.

At first I was quite depressed with the lack of excitement around *The Mother I Carry*. It was really hard to write for publication for quite a while afterward, but then I realized that I had an angel. Maybe every writer gets one that cheers them on in some manner, because you have to have one to survive. But whenever I was in despair about that book—I'd just put my face in my hands instead of write—then my angel arranged for me to receive a letter from a reader of one of my books. It never failed. Right when I was despairing, I'd get a letter and it helped.

*Perhaps the first book was in the right window in the right time. The second book is there when its window comes. The audience that you wrote this book for may not be ready yet. Some books are discovered later.*
I think in some ways, it's a test that all writers go through: to devote a lot of time and energy to something and put it out just trusting that the book will find those who need it. I was very lucky to get *The Mother*

*I Carry* published, which is the first place that people can get knocked down. To deal with it not being what we think of as "successful" made me really evaluate, and go close again to that voice that says, "I must write."

My work has to have meaning. I have to feel it might help or heal. But the "I must write" voice is the one that reminds me that I write for myself, to articulate my own passions and to survive emotionally.

*What happens when you don't write?*
I get stressed out if I don't write. And I get really irritable. I think Julia Cameron says it really well in *The Artist's Way*, when she talks about how on edge people get when they don't create.

I had a big realization about four or five years ago. I'd come home from work and I'd be depressed, and I'd start ranting at Marianne, not yelling at her, but just complaining, "Nothing's ever going to feel right," and, "Nobody cares about what I write," and, "What's the point." I realized that whenever I went into that, what I really needed to do was write.

Really, for all the despair in the rant, I was just trying to make room so that I could write.

When I'm writing, there's a sense of timelessness, spaciousness, and like nothing else is important. Writing itself, when it's appearing, is a remarkable blessing. But sometimes I can hardly get to it for the background hum that says I should be doing something else, I should be making more money, I should be writing faster, I should be writing something that will really sell. And certainly I should return all those e-mails, phone calls, and letters.

*You mean, life pulling at you? The clean-your-refrigerator syndrome?*
Right. For me, it's responding to my correspondence or obligations to other people.

*Where is the critic for you today, when you write? And how much do you worry about being published as you write? Or about audience?*
My critic now is saying that I'm not writing enough, mostly because I

have a novel simmering in my mind and I haven't carved out time to try writing it. But I also have a feeling it's not quite cooked yet. Really, I've become much less self-critical since I've decided to live a non-conventional life. I have a lot of different occupations and I've come to accept that they're all important to me—from seeing a therapy client or giving a massage to making jewelry or giving a lecture and teaching a workshop. I realize that I receive inspiration and can be creative in all these different arenas.

I still need time for writing, but my life is more fluid because mostly I work at home. When I was writing my memoirs, I'd be immersed in writing for eight hours a day, for maybe a month's period. Part of that time I'd be writing in my journal and sobbing, or throwing darts, or playing with my cat. But I would have uninterrupted weeks for writing.

Now, I'm cultivating an approach where I try to validate all aspects of my creativity and find some balance in my lifestyle, so I can write or make a necklace or read or ride my electric bike.

My critic has this really rigid idea, from school and the structure of the workday, I think, that you have to sit down here for eight hours, or six hours, and if you're not doing that you're not really a writer. I have a friend who actually does do that, and I use her sometimes, I project my critic onto her: "Well, Jenny is the one who writes."

*I think there are two "buckets" for writers, we come out of at least two spots: writers who primarily communicate data, and writers who primarily communicate experience. You are particularly interesting because you've grown yourself in both places.*

I'm a technical writer, and I can sit down eight hours a day and write eight hours a day. A journalist can write eight hours a day. They're not usually bringing up as much from the depth. Less is at risk, it is more craft. So it's not as directly personal.

When writing is creative, from synthesizing in the depths of your soul to creating that *room in* that *setting*, or traveling back to a setting in memory and bringing it into your work—anything that involves more of one's self as a channel, or as a conduit, a process—it's wrenching in a different kind of way.

*It's more alchemical. It's less rational. The rational can be furthered by discipline. Creativity requires involvement. For the craft and art of writing, we need both.*

Yes, I think that's true. When I first started my [doctoral] program I wanted to write every day, and I did: I kept a journal even though I had the worst writer's block in my life trying to write my dissertation.

Usually, in order to conceive a long piece, I really need several days where I don't have anything else scheduled. I just read Dickens, where he said if he had some appointment in the day he spent his whole day in worry, and could not write. I thought, "That's me too!" At least I can revise when I have appointments.

Since I've been writing political essays regularly, about subjects I'm quite riled up about, I've been able to write more quickly, though I still need a sense of an open day to work within. The essays have been a great teacher for me because they're about timely, immediate events. I can't let them sit for a month or even a week before I send them out, so I've had the opportunity to let go of my fear of imperfection.

In general I find the hardest part of being a writer trying to find a home for what I write. Every part of this process annoys me a bit: researching the markets, not the revising but the actually getting it perfect and putting it in the envelope, writing a cover letter, that kind of end-task.

That is where I really need my discipline because I'd rather make a necklace or write something else. I can do a lot of that kind of task in a day in which I also have some appointments and am writing some correspondence and things like that, because I can be interrupted. The piece is already born.

But for the birth, it is really useful for me to have a day or two of pretty uninterrupted time.

*When you may or may not be writing.*
Right.

*One author told me that she begins writing by cleaning her house. She used to think that she was avoiding, but she now realizes that this is how she begins.*
I try to start my day with meditating. Of all the practices I've tried, this seems the most useful. Also yoga, and being outside on my bike. I'm still learning to be at home with my own process, and not to try and make other ways fit me if they don't. I want to have my critic come into line with what my process actually is and what I need as a human.

 I had this friend over yesterday, and we wrote together. He is a really new writer, but he's incredibly gifted, he's just so good that it's astonishing. When I called him up, I said, "Why don't you come over on Thanksgiving and we'll write together for an hour?" And he said, "Straight?!" An hour straight for him was something he'd never done. And I was astonished. I'd heard his writing, and what he's done. But he writes very short pieces so far.

*For you, an hour was pushing it because that's not enough.*
Right. It was a very good reminder to my critic that things can be written in all sorts of different ways. What's important is to really follow my own process and to be less hung up in measuring both hours and production.

*Tell me if this is correct: you seem to be increasing your voice range right now, with the kinds of writing you're doing. Yet there is still something in all that which is your voice as a writer. Your approach, how you look at the process of writing, and the way one sees through your writing when we're finished reading it. Where you put the reader's eyes. I don't think your voice is changing or that you're speaking in tongues, as much as that you've trained your voice so well, as a classical writer, in memoirs. And now you're expanding your repertoire. Is that how you see your writing shifting?*
Yes, I think that's true. Probably there are things that will remain pretty consistent because they're of me, throughout what I write.

 One quality can either be called a determination to challenge taboos, which you know I play with a lot, or maybe it's just the natural outgrowth of my lifestyle. Most of what I write seems entirely natural to me, and yet it's outside the mainstream. As far as I can foresee in the future I will probably stay sort of outside the culture and in a challenging position to it. It's just who I am.

The other part of that is that I am a lesbian writer. Being a lesbian is a way I stand, in terms of relationships, and my relationship to women and my relationship to men, that—because I'm a lesbian is a part of my voice. It is distinctive from non-lesbian voices. I can play with the other roles, but there are none so convincing as when I am either writing as a lesbian or writing as a friend.

*Because it comes from values that are deep and authentic to you.*
Yes, I think it is both values and also living those identities. No matter what form my writing takes, it comes from who I am. Writing teaches me about who I am too; it gives me the chance to find out what I really care about, no matter what others currently think.

Writing leads me in certain directions, it enchants me, but it always comes from my personal passion, not from a desire to entertain or to please someone else. Though I do like to make people laugh and cry and feel something of themselves. But the only parts I can control are my willingness to write and also to push it out into the world the best I can.

It is true that for myself I must write. And lately I have also realized how deeply committed I am to putting my work out and being heard, even when it means photocopying it myself and passing it out downtown.

Since I believe that everyone matters, I might as well work at being heard by the people here, where I live. In terms of being heard more globally, that's just luck.

# Regina Barreca

*Speak in tongues, then find your own voice*

### RESEARCH INTERESTS
Feminist criticism, humor, 20th-century British novel, Victorian literature

### PUBLICATIONS INCLUDE
*Too Much of a Good Thing Is Wonderful*
*Perfect Husbands (& Other Fairy Tales): Demystifying Marriage, Men, and Romance*
*Sweet Revenge: The Wicked Delights of Getting Even*
*Untamed and Unabashed: Essays on Women and Humor in British Literature*
*They Used to Call Me Snow White . . . But I Drifted: Women's Strategic Use of Humor*
*The Erotics of Instruction* (editor)
*The Penguin Book of Women's Humor* (editor)
*The Signet Book of American Humor* (editor)
*Sex and Death in Victorian Literature* (editor)

*What is your unique writing voice?*
The voice I write in is the voice that I teach in, which in the most immodest description I could give it, is a bringing together of a lot of the different parts of my life.

I want to talk about *Anna Karenina,* and talk about a *Seinfeld* episode, and talk about the news—all together, without making one seem sacred or the other seem ridiculous, or one seem pathetic—without necessarily saying that something constructed is going to be truer than another thing. I feel very comfortable talking about a whole mixed bag, all at once.

I don't have a different professorial voice than a voice I would use to talk to my girlfriends, and a voice I would use to talk to a hundred people at a business colloquium. People are often surprised to be able to hear all those things put together at once. We're supposed to talk about high culture or low culture or emotional life but not all of them all together. They knock off each other in really interesting ways. The collision of ideas from different parts of life seems to me to make sort of the most interesting results. I see it as one big chemistry experiment. I put these things in and shake them up to see what comes out.

*Is that how you've always spoken or is that something you've grown into?*
Good question. I've pretty much always done it, actually.

My parents were not educated people. Neither of them finished high school. But they were incredibly smart.

My mother was a French Canadian, who converted to being an American, married my father, moved down to Brooklyn, lived with his family for much of her life, died when I was pretty young. And again, she had the French and English editions of *Anna Karenina,* for example, and *Madame Bovary.* All of these books, like *War and Peace,* were supposed to not be read by people with an eighth-grade education, but by people who were much smarter than that.

I learned very early on that education and intelligence are sometimes coincidental but are not causal. If you're smart, you're going to be smart, and you can be educated and that's great, or you can be smart and not educated. You can be stupid and educated, or smart and educated.

But if you're stupid, just because you have an education doesn't mean you're going to be smart. And if you're smart just because you're uneducated doesn't mean you're going to be stupid.

Really knowing that at an early age (as opposed to just knowing it theoretically), it wasn't something that came into question. You could talk about incredibly complex ideas in fairly simple language, without simplifying them, or simplify them but without reducing the complexity of them.

*Or iconizing them?*
Right. Or, using texts or ideas as an initiation rite into something that had to do with class. Being a working-class girl who has had the privilege of having access to this other sort of academic world, I do think it's a privilege. But I certainly wouldn't have wanted to lose where I came from anymore than I've ever attempted to lose my accent.

*How have you had to defend your voice?*
Often. [Laughs] I've had to defend it mostly—not to a popular audience—but to an academic audience. I've been lucky, and I've worked my tail off. I've written a bunch of academic books, and the older I get, and the longer I'm doing this, the less willing I am to speak in an inaccessible, theoretical language that again only a certain number of initiates would be able to read.

I want to write something that everybody would be able to understand. An academic book that I edited (I wrote the introduction and wrote an article) is *The Erotics of Instruction*. It is about student-teacher relationships. I talk about Woolf and Updike, but I also talk about having a crush on my 7th-grade math teacher. Another author who is a lesbian critic wrote an absolutely wonderful essay on growing up and falling in love with everybody in the Hayley Mills movie *No Place for Angels*, a 1960s movie, where the girls are raised by nuns.

The contributors for this book are from across New England. I encouraged all the contributors to write so that everybody is able to read this, even though this is an intellectual and academic debate. I want to be able to send this book to somebody smart who doesn't happen to be doing this [academic debate], or a student who is interested in this, and have them be able to understand it. All of the 18 contributors have done a very good job of making sure that that's the case.

*I'm hearing that in some ways education can become a language barrier? A codification. In order to prove that you have an education, you speak a different kind of language?*
Right. To speak in tongues. [Laughs] A lot of times we tend to use language that's unclear when we don't know what the hell we're talking about.

When I'm speaking to somebody and they say, "Business does this as well as academics," they want me to give a list—during a lecture for instance—of the points you're going to emphasize, or what your goals, objectives, whatever the deal is. They want to discuss your agenda, power, communication, whatever. I sometimes get my stuff rewritten as "We'll make proactive and empower the da da da" and I say, "No, I don't use those words. I'm not interested in that."

What's the difference between "proactive" and "active?" Why is one different from the other? It's like "utilize." Say use. These are good words. We're not savages that need to make like a long series of sounds. If you use language to express an interesting idea that people can hook themselves onto, you don't have to add other kinds of bells and feathers.

*Have you ever tried to write in a falsetto?*
Mm! Yes.

*And what happens to your writing?*
It is like watching videos of yourself dancing with tight shoes, or something. It's really very awkward movement. Looking back at my dissertation, I'm astonished that I was allowed to degree.

*What did you do your dissertation on?*
Good topic: Hate and humor in women's novels.
　　I focused on three 20-century British authors, and had a great time.

But I was sticking in stuff from the Frankfurt school, and things that were really unnecessary for what I was talking about.

But that was part of, in a way, being bilingual. It's like learning another language. To an extent, what I tell my students is, they need to be able to do that. Especially if they're going to do feminist theory, women's literature. They better know their Melville, their Emerson, their Milton, their Proust, and their Tolstoy.

They're going to need to know twice as much. It's like being a foreigner in another country. You have to learn their native tongue. You can't just keep speaking in your own [tongue], otherwise you end up in the ghetto. And if that's what you want, that's fine. If you want to change the infrastructure, then you have to know how to do everything.

*Only in that area? In the feminist theory area?*
I'd like to say that anybody getting their degree on Milton would have to know what Charlotte Bronte did, using Milton, in *Jane Eyre*. It's never, ever going to happen. But if you're going to do something on Jane Eyre, or Charlotte Bronte, you've got to know how Bronte used Milton, because somebody's going to ask you about it, and it's a legitimate question. You cannot say, "Well, Milton is not a woman writer and I don't know how to do it." Because in fact it was important to Bronte, she was using it, and you miss a whole lot of resonance in a text if that is not part of what you've been accustomed to, what you've learned.

We're living in a patriarchal culture. You need to be able to sort of speak in tongues, and then be able to find your own voice.

*Remember your voice. Know how to get home.*
Right, exactly.

*You began by saying that you speak and write in the same voice. In your own identity in your work, are you writer, teacher, or equal parts?*
All together. I would never give up the teaching—I really love teaching—teaching for me very much keeps me honest. I have to keep current, I have to keep reading, they [students] are hungry, it's

exciting—it's contagious. With both writing and teaching, it's a closed loop, in a good way: anything I put out feels like it comes back.

We have to take the world seriously, but not ourselves too seriously. It is a shame that we are willing to accept the artificial categories that divide our work lives from our home lives, or our emotional lives.

We spend so much time at work, all of us. I'm thinking about how much time we spend wondering about our emotional lives and what people think of us, especially dealing with 18 to 22-year-olds. And how little time we spend thinking about our workloads, which are in fact going to take up a lot more waking hours than our love lives ever were. We should be at least worrying as much about what our vocation is going to be as we do about who our partner is going to be. It seems to me a failure that we don't do more of that.

*Did you do that?*
No. Absolutely not. Which is why I feel like I can speak about its importance.

*Keeps you honest.*
Very much. I was driven by this quest for romance. I kept thinking, "If only I could get this right, everything would be fine."

I really backed into the idea of work. My mother was a telephone operator and hated it. When she could stop working, she was delighted. There was not a sense of any kind of accomplishment associated with that. She died when I was 16 so I never got any sense from her about what work life or her ideas for me would be like. She just told me that I should be able to have a job so that if I needed to leave my husband I could. Which she didn't feel like she had. The benefit is, I never felt like I had anybody's pressure on me, and anything I was going to do was going to be fine. [Laughs]

And then to get a scholarship to go to Dartmouth. My relatives had no idea what Dartmouth was. I remember very seriously telling one of my aunts I was going to go to school in New Hampshire, and she paused and said, "You're pregnant, right?" That's the only time anyone left the state, when they got knocked up. I said, "No, I'm not. I got a scholarship." They said, "It's okay. It happened to your cousin, you can come back."

*What is your earliest memory of writing, or, in your case, teaching—communicating?*
Like all kids, I used to make little books. It turns out, that's something a lot of kids do. I remember writing for the elementary school magazine. I did one story about a tiger who seemed very ferocious but was actually toothless—[Laughs] I'm sure Freud could have an interesting time with that one. I was already trying to reassure myself that things were not as scary as they seemed, and humor was one way of doing that.

I think that my family is very funny. Everybody was funny, and that probably was also a nice way to escape from things that were scary or worrying. There were always money troubles; there were always sort of hard times. At least being able to kid about it made it easier.

*Did you have any acknowledgment or support early on for your little books and/or your writing?*
No, not particularly. I guess it was probably good that I was playing quietly. Maybe many writers started out that way. But I think it was my brother, if anybody, that was supposed to be the writer in the family.

*Is he [a writer]?*
No. I dedicated a book to him. He is an excellent writer. He's six years older than I am, and he's just finishing law school. He works full time. Three kids. It is almost as if we swapped lives. I bet that if my mother had predicted something for each of us, she would have predicted that he would have been a writer and a teacher, and I would have been working, with three kids, and living in Brooklyn.

And so it was an interesting thing, somewhere along the way, going to each other, "Huh, I got your script somehow, I don't know how this ended up." I think we're okay about it, with envy on both sides. I adore his family, I think it's wonderful. And I think he wishes he had my job. It is nicely even. We're both probably getting better and sort of easier with our lives as we get older. I just turned 40 this year. And that feels very good. I'm really looking for the next ten years to be calmer and certainly better, easier than the ten years before.

When I got divorced I was on my own and I was afraid of being alone, but I'm not afraid of words. I have always felt words have been my friends, my allies. They are the balls that I juggle. They are protection and weapon and tool and all at once.

*You mentioned one strategy of making sure you know as many languages as possible, in order to continue to use that power of words. Are there any other ways in which you have had to defend, protect?*
I sometimes talk to all-male groups. I get 200 guys from the insurance industry; they've been told that they're going to listen to somebody talk about humor, because I fill their anti-harassment quota. For me it's the equivalent of hunting, I guess. I really want to strap the ones who start to laugh to the hood of my car; I'm so delighted at their conquest. I feel like I'm colonizing a place when I can get them to laugh, and I've been very lucky.

In fact the only group I couldn't get to laugh was a group of women in [a wealthy New York City suburb] who were very fancy, and I mean perfectly nice—they bought all the books. But they didn't laugh. Maybe their jaws were wired shut or something—they just couldn't—no expressions. It was very frightening. It was like the *Stepford Wives*. That is when I was very glad that I get paid to speak because I could just take my check. I was standing near the exit.

The ability to get somebody to laugh really is about getting somebody on your side. Once they've laughed with you, it's really hard not to have some kind of association with your side of it. So if you've got them, and they can admit it, they don't feel like they've laughed against their will or something, then you're standing briefly on the same side so you have a similar perspective.

And that's great. For all of the things that are very very different in life, there are moments when we don't see exactly the same thing, but we can at least see the same side of something. I'm delighted to have that happen. I'm not resentful of that, I don't find it scary, I don't feel there should be some kind of separation, I don't think there's a big wall.

And also, women need to learn how to get what has often been the private articulate discussion, exploration of emotion and ideas, into the public. We need to be able to do that, it's our responsibility. That means accepting the possibility of failure. We were girls, so we've been encouraged to accept the possibility of failure—failure is not unfamiliar to all too many of us. What really scares a lot of us, is that people don't like us. And that's going to happen too.

You open your mouth; someone is not going to like you. And you talk to 20 people, you talk to 50 people, you—somebody's going to get mad, to feel you're bossy, somebody's going to feel you have a big mouth, somebody's going to be upset. And that's okay. You are not going to make anybody like you anyhow. Why say, "But if I say something like that, they're going to think I'm a bitch. They're going to think I'm trying to take over. They're going to think it's like . . ." And your point is? Yes? Okay, now it's up to you; why do you care?

*Could this be your next book, please?*
I'm talking about women who have already taken a lot of risks and put themselves out there, who are still afraid they're going to say [gasp], "I sent that memo, and it didn't go to this one." If we could only harness the time that we had spent double-thinking everything that we think, say, and do, as to whether or not we're going to hurt somebody's feelings. Part of it is compassion, a lot of it is paranoia. And a lot of it is again, a reluctance, that's fostered by the culture, of women to take responsibility for our lives.

Part of not being objectified and done to, not being the passive creature, is to take responsibility for screwing up, for making somebody mad, for all of those things. That means also that you can't yell at everybody else for doing that to you. Because they're not: you're doing it yourself. And that's robbing some people of an escape route that has become—not maybe comfortable—but at least familiar.

There are students who will always do a paper at the last minute, and say, "Well, if I had had another week on this it really could have been good, but here." What that allows them to do is to avoid the idea that maybe the best they are is a B student. If they're always doing something under pressure they never have enough time, they never—whatever the deal is, then they never have to face that they're really good or they're really not that good. There is this nice little fiction that's reassurance, "If you don't put yourself on the line all the time, then you could be better."

Rita Mae Brown has a wonderful quote in the beginning of *Southern Discomfort*. A wonderful little Note to the Reader. It says, "If you don't like my book, write your own. If you don't think you can write a novel, that ought to tell you something. If you think you can, then do it. No excuses. If you still don't like my novels, find a book you do like. Life is too short to be miserable. If you like my novels, I commend your good taste."

It is just wonderful, it's saying, "Before you open your mouth, you better be able to figure out what it is that you need to do yourself before you criticize." I love that sense of challenge—the put-up-or-shut-up sort of idea.

I tell students, "If you're going to write you have to read." Especially in school, the teachers as well as students get so wrapped up in preparing for what you're doing, you don't read.

*For your books, do you write them as you go along? Or do you structure them out?*
No. I know where I'm going, and when I'm writing I set myself a real schedule that I stick to. I'm good with my self-imposed deadlines. And I take criticism really well.

*But it's clear that you don't stretch a point.*
Good. I hope not. I pay attention, so that I see a lot coming together. In the best parts of the book those are the things that happen. Where things you wouldn't necessarily put together sort of turn out to come together.

*And there's energy as you read when that's happening.*
Yes, that's because that's the fun part when I'm writing. I choose pretty broad canvases—you can talk about revenge forever. Or marriage or

relationships, there's just no stopping. There's an arbitrary point at which you just have to stop writing a book and turn it in, and that's what finishes that, not because the topic is exhausted. If I were going to do "symbolism of fire in 18th-century literature," the people who do that well, do that with as much enthusiasm and energy as taking these incredibly big places, but that's all they do. They have the one idea and they keep going on it.

*I don't want to skim your books, because I know there's going to be a surprise. Do you plant it there, or if you are surprised when you get there too?* It is like a running conversation. I sit down at the computer and I have a sense of who my readers are, especially after *They Used to Call Me Snow White . . . But I Drifted*. I got comfortable, talking to women my age. "My age" is now anybody who is too old for work-study and too young for Medicare: 18 to 60.

In our most intimate lives, we have incredibly similar experiences. We get our buttons pushed because the culture has planted those buttons, so they know how to push them. They know how to get us going in one direction or another and it's such a relief for me to feel like I can make use of those.

The original title for *They Used to Call Me Snow White . . . But I Drifted* was *Is That a Pistol in Your Pocket*? (a Mae West line). And the publisher said, "That's too aggressive." And I said, "If you think the title's too aggressive, you don't know what's coming."

# Megan LeBoutillier

*I write the books I need to read*

### GENRE
Creative nonfiction

### PUBLICATIONS INCLUDE
*Little Miss Perfect*
*"No" Is a Complete Sentence*

*Describe your writing voice.*
Oftentimes my writing voice is that of a child. Or it starts out as the voice of a child, who's trying to find something out. As time has progressed, my writing voice has become much more confident in what I have to say, and a lot less fearful about the process of going places if I'm not really sure where we're going to end up.

*The confidence has changed over time. Has the process changed over time?*
Oh, absolutely. When I first started writing with the intention of being a writer, as opposed to being a journal keeper or complainer or whatever else writing was for me, it was agonizing. I thought there was a

prescription for writing, and a way that it was supposed to be done. What I seemed to be doing didn't fit that model of what I thought I was supposed to be doing. I had a tremendous struggle with that.

I struggled a lot, to allow, to make Megan listen to what Megan was writing. That struggle is pretty much over with now. Being in school [Union] now, I have the obedient student, what-the-teacher-expects-of-me writer. I have the oh-let-me-tell-you-about-my-experience Megan-the-writer.

We had to write a paper for this seminar, and I read the question, and immediately the struggle started to happen between the obedient student and "What do they want to hear," and Megan—who had a story to tell, who was going to illustrate the point that they asked without using any of that language that was in the question. And so there's a struggle there.

In general, I don't have nearly the agony of letting my voice come out that I had ten, twelve years ago when I first got started.

*You talked about the difference between writing, or being a writer versus a journal keeper? The difference being, for you . . . ?*
Well, the first thing that pops into my head is an audience. I mean, no one was intended to see my journals. And *audience*, I'm going to say, is the difference. I always had a dream that I wanted to be a writer, which in my mind meant that you wrote something, books presumably, that other people would read.

I stopped doing that public kind of writing when my childhood attempts at it got found, and were scrutinized in a rather critical manner by my mother. I was unable to defend them. So I stopped doing that kind of writing, that might have an intended audience. I just went underground and wrote in my diary, or wrote journals that were for me only.

*You touched on two questions that I have: how have you had to defend your voice, and what is your earliest memory of writing?*
As a child, around eight, I wrote stories in a kind of ritualistic manner with colored pencils and ribbon. I imagine, looking back on it, they were

thinly veiled renderings of what was going on in my household, which was fairly chaotic and not particularly understandable to a child. Now that I've had some psychology courses I understand what that was about, but at the time, I couldn't defend what I was doing and I hid the work.

I came home from school one day and my mother had found it. It was all laid out on my bed and she was standing there going, "What is this?" I didn't have anything to tell her about what it was, so I felt ashamed. I tore it all up and I threw it away and that was the end of my story writing.

And that was the end of Megan, showing up in a public way with her writing.

In the fourth or fifth grade, my English composition teacher wrote in the margin of my paper, "You don't seem to put any of yourself into your work," and I thought, "Hooray! I have managed to successfully erase myself," which was exactly what I intended to do. To this day I don't know whether that was an objection or a compliment to the work. That person also never came to me and said, "Gee, wouldn't you like to bring some of yourself into the writing?" So I just assumed that that was a check like, "Yes, you're doing this right."

I continued to not show up in my written work for school, forever. So, that, I think, answers one of your questions.

*The other question was about defense.*
I never wanted to be in a position again to have to defend myself, so I didn't put myself in there. Anytime the work might be scrutinized by somebody, I didn't show up.

*Now that your work is published, now that Megan is in print, have you had to defend your voice?*
No. My family pretty much totally ignored my first book. I don't even know what they tell people I do. At my brother's wedding, my mother's friends were approaching me and talking to me with what appeared to be the understanding that I was a psychologist.

So, [laughs] I don't [have to defend my voice], and critically, if there's been any review of my work I've not seen it.

I've had a fairly easy time getting my work into print. I have a third book that isn't finding its way into print quite so easily, but I certainly haven't been in a position to have to defend anything. I have the fear every time I send a paper . . . or an application to [a school or for a fellowship], any time I put myself into work like that and send it out, I have fear, not that I'm going to have to defend it but that it's going to be ignored or criticized or something. It's getting better, it's a much safer environment for the writer in me now than it used to be.

*Your family had no reaction to your book?*
Not that came to me. There may have been some reaction but it didn't come to me.

*That's amazing.*
[Laughs] Family alcoholism is a pretty amazing disease in what it can manifest or not manifest. I imagine some of them have some feeling about it, but they didn't ever tell me. Part of me really believes that none of them ever read it.

*How did you pick your genre?*
It picked me. [Laughs] Believe me, I had every intention, because—oh I've forgotten someone else who was an early influence. My high school English teacher, Mrs. Katz, pronounced in English class one day that the only real writing was poetry and fiction.

So, naturally, when I was going to be "a writer," I wanted to do *real* writing. Poetry was ruined early on in school for me; poetry never seemed like what it was going to be. So I was going to be a fiction writer. And I was going to be a Virginia Woolf or Eudora Welty, or somebody who was very good at it.

When I started writing, [fiction] was not what started to come out. And I just tried and tried and tried and tried to make that come out. It was a long time before I got out of my way and realized *this* flows [gestures to the right], and *this* doesn't [gestures to the left]. And I didn't know what *this* [gestures again to the right], what I did, was called.

I knew that *this* [to the left], what I called fiction, didn't flow. So I finally just decided, "Well, let's listen to what it is that you have to say, what just comes out of you easily. Let's not worry about the name of the genre, and if it's justified. Let's just see what comes out."

I hadn't known what to call it until I started in the Union program and I discovered creative nonfiction. And then it was like, "Oh yes, yes, yes, yes, that's a name that fits for me." I was real stuck on genre separation, and what was legitimate and what wasn't legitimate.

I'm pretty much throwing all of that away these days, deciding that writing is writing. I'm trying to get Mrs. Katz out of my head but she's still in there to some degree.

*What role has silence played in your writing?*
Wow. Well, I think of the time when my mother found the stories and laid them on my bed as a creative wound—that that effectively silenced my public voice.

While the struggle was really intense to get back to my writing voice and I railed against that, I'm so thankful that I had to fight as hard as I had to fight to get back in touch with my creative self. It has really turned out to be a gift in the long run, because I wouldn't have fought so hard for something that came easily. So that's one kind of silence, that's the *verb*, silence.

*"You wouldn't have fought so hard for something that came easily"? So having been stifled, is this like Woody Allen not wanting to belong to a club that would have him as a member?*
No, I don't think it's that. I think it wouldn't have been as meaningful.

I don't play the piano very easily; it's too hard for me and I'm not that interested in being a piano player, so I don't bother with it. But being a writer is a lifelong dream, and somewhere along the line I realized that I had released the dream—or been separated from it or something. At some point it became very important that I get back in touch with that dream.

And I sort of appreciate now being on the other side of the struggle, that I really had to work very hard for something.

*Can you give me a sense of the ages [of the struggle]? You said your mother had your things laid out on your bed when you were—*
Eight. And when I was 28, I started really actively re-engaging with myself as a writer, or trying to.

*Was there any precipitating incident that led to . . .*
[Laughs] Yes, of course. I was trying to finish college. I was 28, I had fought my way through traditional education colleges and generally in the door one semester and out the door at the end of it.

Traditional education and I were ruined for one another when I was in high school. I found a program called the Adult Degree Program at Vermont College—a learner-directed program, not unlike Union. I went to my first residency, ten days, absolutely certain that I was going to do a straight psychological study about families and alcoholism. I came home after ten days up there with a study plan that said that I was going to write short pieces of fiction! I don't really know what happened [laughs], but I thought, "Well, trust *process*." And I did.

Eighteen months later, after an agonizing six months of trying to write short pieces of fiction, and realizing all kinds of interference and distortion in my own mind, my second six-months' study with [Vermont] was an autobiographic journal-writing segment, in which I separated out and identified multiple internal personalities that I named and made very specific and real in my life.

I orchestrated dialogue between them, I used them. And figured out just what all the hum had been in my mind for years.

Then, my third six-months, I used those characters to describe a process of trying to get back in touch with my creative process.

That was the book about families and alcoholism. And I was in the book this time, because I belonged in the book, from the very first, and so the whole thing kind of went full circle.

*Was that* No! Is a Complete Sentence?
No, that was *Little Miss Perfect*. Little Miss Perfect is one of my sub-personalities. My search was to get back in touch with my creativity and something was blocking it. I had a feeling that it had to do with

perception distortion as a result of being told that what you saw happening wasn't really happening, which goes on in alcoholic families, and in my family. The process reconnected me and I was back on track.

Even after that manuscript got me a college degree and then was sold and became a book, I didn't think I was a writer, because I still hadn't written fiction. I'd written two books, and I still didn't believe I was a writer.

Now that I'm in the Union Institute & University and I have somebody who keeps saying, "What you do is legitimate writing," I'm beginning to believe I'm a writer. But [laughs] I haven't totally achieved legitimacy yet. In my own mind. But, I'm better. I'm closer.

No! Is a Complete Sentence *came after* Little Miss Perfect?
Yes. I jokingly say I write the books I need to read, but it's really not a joke. That is what directs my research, and my questioning. I need to understand and to unravel certain things that seem to be knotted up in my life.

My journey doesn't seem to be all that off from what other people might be struggling with. And so then, the book.

*What is your next book?*
The one that's trying to find a publisher right now is called *The Awareness of Possibility*. I think it's my best work, but I'm having more trouble getting this one in print. Not really trouble, it's just not happening as quickly and easily.

As one agent told me, "Howard Stern's book is on the best-seller list, what can I tell you?" And I said, "I think you've lost the vision of this book. Why don't you send the manuscript back." It's a strange market, you know. It's a strange market.

*You couldn't be writing about those [Harold Stern's] kinds of possibilities?*
No, I'm not! At all! But that's what sells right now. And that's what agents look at: what sells.

*What has been your brick wall, your nemesis, in writing?*
Legitimacy. You know, whether or not what I was doing was legitimate writing. And I constantly suspect that it isn't. And I don't know why I care, but I do.

*There's no one in the sub-personality cast who can accept that legitimacy that is all over your work? Or in accepting it, do you lose something?*
If there is a sub-personality that can accept it, she has a very short-term memory, because she doesn't hold onto it for very long.

*To accept legitimacy or an accomplishment would be to frighten some sub-personality who survives by accomplishment?*
Yes, Little Miss Perfect doesn't want to know that she's gotten there, because then she will not have any reason to exist! [Laughs]

Little Miss Perfect, by the way, is just so thrilled we've entered the Union Institute! It revived her, to some extent. Rather than having to be very careful with where she can and cannot be, she's very good for getting stuff done, like a Union program.

But when it comes time to make dinner, or have a relationship with another human being, I have to put her back in the box.

*Your writing process now: do you have times and ways in which you write?*
I'm still a journal-keeper, and I have a regular practice with that. I am trying to experiment with some different ways of doing it.

I try very hard to have Tuesdays and Thursdays be the day that I stay home, and I don't go anywhere and I turn the phone off. And it's *just* about writing. Only if I just really cannot, cannot, *cannot* write anything will I let myself read. The rest of the time it's just hit and miss.

I'm trying to make two full days when I get the writing part done.

*Can you write for eight hours straight? (Megan shakes her head no) Ten hours straight? (Megan shakes her head no again) No?*
No. Going to the kitchen, nervously eating, [laughs] washing the dishes, doing the laundry. I can be with it better than I used to be able

to. If I knew that I really wanted to get myself to start writing, I would do everything in the world but.

Because I have distinct things to do right now [in The Union doctoral program] and I know what they are—and some of them have an actual beginning and an end—that helps lower the anxiety that I feel about writing most of the time. Also it's costing me a lot of money to *not* do it. I think those things are helping to motivate, getting the writing done more.

When I've just been working on book projects and stuff, I will procrastinate for a long time sometimes. I always tell myself that the work is just *cooking*, but that's not altogether true. [Laughs] So I'm liking that discipline is getting better, and my clarity is getting better in my work. Having way way way way way! too much of it to do helps to get it done....

What I'm finding is (I do this with cooking too), the work just begins to inform what the paper is going to be. I had to tell my mother one time that I don't know what I'm going make out of this (food), because the food just starts to inform me about what it's going to become a little bit before dinnertime.

I'm glad that's happening, because it seems like a miracle. If I'd planned it, then I wouldn't want to do it. So it's just kind of coming out of my imagination, which I think is probably the best place for it to be coming out of.

*If you were going to give a sentence about your identity, where would "writer" be in it?*
Oh, it would be in the first few words. I am a writer. [Laughs] I am a writer. I don't tell people anything else first before that.

I'm always surprised by what that seems to say to people. There are people who take me immediately and put me up on some really high pedestal, where I'm just like, "Hah! Get over it!" Or, it makes me so legitimate in their eyes that I feel like a real impostor about it. Or else, they just kind of step away from it, like I just told them I was a leper. They don't really know what to say next.

I don't know what they think. There are people who I recognize simply don't relate to that as an answer to their question of "What do you do?" They can't figure out how I spend my days, or where I go to do it. They don't have a point of intersection with that . . .

*Or how dangerous it is?*
Or how frightening it is. So, they step away from it.

*Is there anything else that I haven't asked you that you'd like to say?*
We talked a lot about legitimacy. And I just thought of this, when I was saying that people don't intersect with it: not having a real job, what looks like a real job to other people, not having children and a husband, all the things that I think make somebody a legitimate person.

Writing is the hardest work I think there is to do but nobody ever sees you doing it. Most of the people in my town who see me around think that I don't do anything. And I probably look like somebody who doesn't do anything. I don't wear clothes that look like I went to the office that day and I can show up at the post office at 11:30 or I can show up at 4:00 in the afternoon, times of day when other people are busy.

That plays into the whole legitimacy piece about what you do. If I could stick my books to my ears, and say, "This is what I do"—but I feel vulnerable to other people's judgments sometimes.

I think of the man who gives me my mail—if I have a slip in my post office box, he always says, "Oh, so what are we doing today? Eating bon-bons?" And it hurts me. He has no idea what I do. He has no idea of what my identity is, and that kind of hurts my feelings.

Writing for me was never about getting famous. But it also had something to do with not remaining invisible, and not remaining silent.

I find I'm embarrassed when I show up with the work. I like sending my books out and having them be away from me and being able to tell people things but not having to be present.

There is still some sort of separation between Megan-the-person and Megan-the-writer and Megan-who-did-this-work-that-is-this-book. I don't really know if I'm explaining that all that well, but it hasn't integrated perfectly yet. If there is a perfect integration. I don't know.

*You said you'd always wanted to be a writer, from very little on?*
Yes, I think I was born knowing that I wanted to tell stories. Or hear stories, or be around stories. When I was an undergraduate in college, I wasn't writing poetry or fiction, so I certainly wasn't going to do anything in English. I was an anthropology major, because I loved the stories and I loved knowing how people created their world and what stories they told to each other. I thought, "That's what I was supposed to be involved in."

Later on I was into psychology because I was trying to clean up some of my own house, and again, there are stories there. It is curious and interesting kinds of information.

When I applied to Union, I had this project that I was going to write, that I thought was under the heading of social psychology. Union sent my application to a psychologist and a writer, who led me through some questions and helped me to identify that my field is actually creative nonfiction. What I like to do is research and write books about things that interest me. It hadn't occurred to me to call that *writing*.

*When you were a child, did you tell stories?*
I wrote those stories [that her mother discovered] when I was real little. I honestly don't remember exactly what those stories were about. After I stopped writing them, I sure read stories. I was a kid that read books constantly. Books were my friends and my escape place.

I also was a mini-librarian in my own home. I set up my personal bookshelves as a library. I had little borrowing cards in them. Nobody came to my library, but I had this ritual around books, and it's served me very well. I'm finding I do the same thing now!

I have always had a relationship with books, and pens and pencils and paper and all the trappings of *Writer*. I've always had a desk, and a typewriter, and I've always had the look of a writer's life. I just didn't always do the *work* of writing.

*Did you have a special place where you would write when you were a child? Do you have a special place now?*
I have a special place—well, not a *special* place, I have a place where the computer is.

*For your journal writing, do you write anywhere?*
Yes, that roams. I don't remember, as a kid. Probably my room. I had my own room, and my room was my safe place.

When I go back and read my journals, from those years, when I think of myself as being silenced, I was putting words on paper, but the content was like, zip. The year my parents got divorced, my journal would skip about two weeks and never mention it. Then there's "President Kennedy was shot today, and I washed my hair and David Bow looked at me." There are words, but there is nothing going on.

*And how old were you then?*
Eight. I know that my parents getting a divorce was a very significant event and I didn't mention it. At the time, I was told not to mention it. My father told us they were getting a divorce, and then we had a birthday party and friends came over to the house for lunch. We were not allowed to tell them. Then my father packed all of his birthday presents and everything in his car and moved to a hotel.

That's how my family dealt with announcing the dissolution of our family as it had been up until that point. And you're surprised I didn't mention it [laughs] in my book!?

I don't think really until I got to be an adolescent did anything of any particular content start being put into my journals. By that point, I wasn't living at home anymore. So I had the illusion of some privacy. I went to boarding school.

After about 13 I pretty much didn't ever go home again. I went home on vacations but I'd spend as little time there as possible. The thing that really I sometimes feel sadness and some anger about, was that nobody ever took me aside and said, "You're really a bright girl, what do you want to do with your life?"

*Not even at boarding school?*
Nowhere. Nowhere. My writing *never* got noticed, which I think probably it shouldn't have. At that point, I had blanded it down to such a point that it was intended to not be noticeable. I was invisible and I mean we were just getting by. Other than that I was a really bright girl, they gave me good grades, but they never encouraged me in any particular area or asked me what I was interested in or what would I like to be, or do.

*Would you have told them?*
*Could* I have told them? I don't think so, I don't know.

I honestly don't think I figured out what I wanted to be when I grew up until about a year and a half ago. [Laughs] I'm not even sure I'm totally on beat with it right now, but: a *real* writer!

If I have a Ph.D. in creative writing, by God, I think maybe I will be able to at least hit myself in the head with it from time to time and tell myself, "I'm a real writer."

# Rachel Vail

*Permission not to have to be Mozart*

**GENRE**

Young adult, children's fiction

**PUBLICATIONS INCLUDE**

| | |
|---|---|
| Sometimes I'm Bombaloo | (*Friendship Ring* Series) |
| Over the Moon | Fill in the Blank |
| Mama Rex & T (series) | If You Only Knew |
| Daring to Be Abigail | Not That I Care |
| Ever After | Please, Please, Please |
| Wonder | Popularity Contest |
| Do-Over | What Are Friends For? |

*Please describe your writing voice.*
I try to leave my characters' fingerprints all over the work. I come from a theater background, so the way I approach creating a character is very similar to the way an actor begins. I try to find who my character is physically. Have you heard the phrase "where the character's center is?" I try to figure out where the character holds her weight, how the

character sits, where she clenches when she's tense, what she does with her fingers when she's nervous, how she stands when she feels confident, and how she stands when she's feeling awkward. I try to get inside the physicality of my character.

Then I try to figure out as much about the background, particularly of my narrator, but really of every character in the book. I know all about their history, what they wanted to be when they were younger, what's the thing that I regret having done, what do I worry about, what's the first thing I think people notice about me as a character? Before I can write from the point of view of a character, I feel like I need to become her. And, so far at least, each of my characters has been very different. I try to build that in a very organic way, before I begin the writing process.

Then, since in order to have any drama you need an antagonist as well, I'll try to do that whole same process with at least the major five or ten characters in the book.

I write from the point of view of adolescents. I need to know what did her mom want to be when she grew up? What were her hopes and her disappointments? What was the dating situation between her parents and how old was she when she had this kid? What was her relationship with her parents? I go through her whole history, everything, so that I know very in-depth who each of my characters is.

*Do you write out a profile on each of them?*
Much of it. I write on a computer, and it's all sort of Socratic, asking questions. It's sort of like a journal on my own, other than the forms that form a character. My mother is a psychologist. From different psychological sentence-completion questionnaires that she uses, I took what were the most illuminating questions and also added some others of my own. I fill out these questionnaires, doing sentence-completion tests for my characters. Those change over time, but I often will start with something like that.

*When you get into the physicality of them, for instance in* Wonder, *did you, like an actor, walk around in Jessica (the narrator)?*
Oh yes, I walked around in Jessica. I went to the grocery store in Jessica. I walked around the apartment in Jessica. I would go to the refrigerator and say, as Jessica, "What do I feel like eating? Nothing!"

*Did you get a Wonder dress?*
I didn't. [Laughs] But that actually came out of a shopping experience with my mother. I was having trouble figuring out specifically what it was that would set Jessica apart. I was feeling frustrated that the work wasn't being as specific as I wanted it to be right then. So I was stomping around as Jessica, and my mom asked if I would go shopping with her. I said, "I guess." I stomped through the store with her. She was very sweet, and very supportive.

*She knew you were—?*
She did not know I was being Jessica. She thought she was shopping with me. Instead she was shopping with 12-year-old Jessica. She would hold up a shirt, "Oh, you know, I think we'll buy you something," and she held up a sweater, "Oh, this is cute!" And I said, "Yeah, it looks like a Wonder Bread explosion." And she said, "Okay," and put it down, and went on to something else.

    Then Rachel clicked in and thought, "Yes, that's it!" And then made lists of "Well, okay, so she could wear that stupid sweater, and somebody could say, 'It looks like a Wonder Bread explosion,' and maybe it's better if it's a dress and other kids are in jeans, and then maybe, no, not designer jeans, that's been done," and then it's lists!

*So your director/author then comes in . . .*
Right. So then I said, "That's it, that's it!" and my mother said, "What, the sweater? Did you want—shall we get this sweat—" "No! Let's go, let's go, let's go!" She put down her things that she had chosen to try on, and came racing out of the store with me. I said, "I'll explain later," and went running down to my office and wrote it. A very rudimentary draft of 15 [pages] is what came out of that.

I walk around often as my characters. Just last week I was doing a school visit, and I walked into the cafeteria as my latest character, Zoe. Not with a specific scene in mind, just as Zoe, walking into the cafeteria. I let the smells hit me, and also the feeling of, "I don't know which table to sit in," and, "Nobody is asking me to come over," and, "I'm going to be all alone," and, "What if I drop my tray?" All those thoughts rush in for a few seconds. Who knows? That's usable sometime. So are my fingerprints all over it? Yes, but I am trying to be Jessica, or whoever.

*Do you write a set and scene putting an outline together that way, or does that come as you're writing it?*
I'm writing a series right now. What I've done before is: I know that the beginning of the story is when the character's world is turned upside-down—when everything changes for the character. The crisis will come when this character that I'm in the midst of creating, the fatal flaw, or the situation, the paradox within the character, comes to a choice, comes to a head. I know that that's where it ends. Usually I know which way I think the character's going to choose to resolve it. So far, I've plotted out where I think it's going to end.

The most dramatic change was in *Daring to Be Abigail*, which takes place in camp. I outlined it very loosely, and had plotted it out through the whole summer: what would happen, how she would eventually succeed in overcoming her doubts about herself, all of that.

Abigail defined herself from the beginning as someone who never says "no" to a dare. She feels like her father didn't think that she was a courageous person, and her father died a couple of years ago. So she's come to camp sort of like a quest, to redefine herself, to try out being somebody she thinks her father would like better. She sets herself up as somebody who never says "no" to a dare. Then she's dared to do something truly dreadful, to another girl in the bunk[house]—a girl who she actually likes, although the girl is an annoying person in some ways, too.

Abigail is dared to do it, and she does it. She does this horrible thing. Most books for adolescents come to the climax of "Do the right thing or cave in." In most of the books that I've read, the kid chooses to do the right thing and then her community rallies around her and sees that she has done the right thing.

What I did with the three books leading up to it, I think, like with *Wonder*—push comes to shove for Jessica when she's there in the store, and she has to lash out at Sheila and she can't quite bring herself to. Now, the community doesn't rally around her and say, "Yes, it is better to all be nice." In fact, things fall apart a bit for Jessica from then on.

In my first three books, the kid has come to the crisis and against what she feels like she should do, she stands up—she or he—does really what I think of as "the right thing." And it doesn't make it easy. The denouement is not: "Everyone rallies round and thinks you're a great person." They, like Huck Finn, have to do what their good core told them to do, despite the repercussions.

In *Daring to Be Abigail*, Abby does the wrong thing. She knows that it's wrong while she's doing it. She knows it's a bad thing, but she does it anyway, and suffers the consequences. So, a little bit different.

*One of my questions is: how has your writing voice changed over time?*
Well, I guess that's one way.

*The moral complexity increases.*
I'm hoping that [is so]; I don't know if it's true. I'm hoping that as I go on, I'll become more and more honest. My aim is to be totally honest about how it feels to be an adolescent: how it feels to be Jessica, or how it feels to be Zoe. For me that takes a lot of rewriting; because of the complexity of the layers of emotions in my characters, I revise and learn as I go along. The books may become more morally complex. But I hope more truthful, too.

*How did you pick this genre?*
It's funny, because it gives me pimples sometimes.

*Gives you pimples?*
I really think it's the kind of things that *they* go through is what gives them the pimples, and I have to live through it! Over and over.

A great playwriting teacher of mine in college told me, "Drama is in the pinnacle moments of life, the life-or-death situation." I am not as interested in writing thrillers about "What do you do when the guy's gun is sticking into your face"—that doesn't reflect my reality.

In junior high school, walking down the hall can feel like life or death. Nobody sitting with you at lunch is about as dreadful a feeling to a 12-year-old as any kind of ostracizing is to an adult, because that's what it is—exclusion from your whole world.

Adolescents are suddenly having adult feelings without any adult perspective. They can feel passion for the first time, or attraction, or depression—but have no idea that sometimes this happens. Whereas, an adult will say, "Oh, that's funny, I guess I'm attracted to that guy, oh well, it's happened a hundred times before," and you barely notice it. But the first time it happens, you think, "Oh my God! I must be in love! I've never felt this way! What if I feel like this from now on?" Every moment can be so full of drama that I can underplay, rather than become operatic about it.

*Yes. I really enjoyed reading* Wonder, *because I remembered what adolescence is like. And it felt that you were giving permission, allowing your characters to have these experiences and emotions, so mercurial and conflicted and sometimes so confusing. I imagined being a teenager, reading that and just feeling relief, in reading it, and wondered how you were able to recapture that.*

I'll say two ways—acting and stubborn memory.

I remember very clearly being 7, and being 12. I was small, and I've always looked young for my age. I had very strong opinions, and definite beliefs, and I would voice my beliefs. People would say, "Oh! She's so precocious!"

And I remember mostly yelling, "That just means short!" [Laughs]

I swore to myself as a kid: "I will remember this," and I said over and over again, "If they only knew how complex my life is, and how deep my feelings are, how much I'm going through, they would never condescend to me the way that they do."

I always felt very wary of anybody condescending to me, probably because I was small.

I made a decision to remember things, so that if I someday had kids, I would really listen to them and would take them seriously. I would know that at 14, you can be in love, and at 12, you can have opinions about a Presidential election, and know what you want! And even if that knowledge changes the next day, you knew it then—definitely. That was part of it.

The other part is, through my acting training, I learned to use sense memories. One thing I used in the book *Ever After*.

I picked up a rubber band that was on my desk and I closed my eyes. It's an acting exercise: hold an object, and smell it, feel it, and see where you go with it. As I smelled the rubber band, I could smell the smell of newsprint and old coffee. I remembered being in my dad's old blue Rambler, and going with him to get bagels on Sunday morning. Then I remembered the sound of my feet on the floor and the scratching of the dirt on the floorboards. My dad always said, "The only thing holding this car together is the dirt!" but my mom used to bug him to get the car washed.

This led to a scene with Molly and her father, which felt very true, because it had all those elements. I had tapped into something I had really forgotten until I brought it back with smell.

*That's one of the ways you bring that voice back?*
Right.

Molly is very different from me in some ways, so I then had to change it to her and her father.

*What role has silence played in your writing?*
Silence. You mean in the characters' lives or in my office?

*Anything from being silenced to how you use silence.*
Right. It's an interesting question, in that way. My home growing up was very warm and loving, and I was never silenced. My parents always

sought out my opinions. I was encouraged to tell stories and to have opinions. My father played the piano, my mother is a soprano, and we were the Vail Family Singers. There was always noise and laughter and singing. Only at bad times, tense times, was it silent. So I probably have a fear of silence.

When I talk about Jessica's family (and it is a hyperbolic family, where everybody's sort of yelling and hugging and laughing, the brother is throwing things), that's my happy family, even when she's going through bad things.

In *Do-Over*, Whit is very much the opposite of Jessica [from *Wonder*]: where she's explosive, he's implosive. When things go badly, he turns it inside himself, says, "It's all right," and goes outside and plays basketball. His home is silent. His parents don't explode at each other—when they communicate at all, it's quiet jabs. That to me is very scary.

Also the silence between Molly and her parents I guess is troubling to her—funny, I hadn't thought of it as a theme through my books—and maybe even with Abigail, the silence of the father not being there anymore—when she thinks of happy times, when her father was alive, they're raucous, fun times, and she misses his laugh.

*And Sheila and Jessica had a silence. They weren't talking.*
Right. To me, words, communication, is a *sine qua non* of existence, or at least of happiness. The silent treatment is a spooky thing to me.

In the book I'm writing right now, the main character is the youngest of five, and her house is very loud, and constant commotion. This is a series; it will be sort of an ongoing exploration. She's discovering a place of silence inside herself that she's covered up with all this noise and hasn't allowed herself to explore at all.

*Nice. What is your earliest memory of writing or communicating?*
Hmm. Of writing, well, I remember that in second grade I was a poet. In fact, I found my second-grade teacher and she recognized me, because I have the same haircut, she said.

*Now?*
Apparently. Time to update.

She asked me if I was still writing. This was soon after *Wonder* had been published. I said, "Yes, actually I'm a writer," and she said, "Oh! A poet?" I said, "No, you know it's been a while since I wrote poetry." But after second grade I didn't think of myself at all as a writer. But I did write. I remember sitting very moodily, in the window of my dad's office, in second grade, and writing a poem about darkness. Feeling very existential, as only a seven-year-old can.

I guess I can't remember a time when I wasn't telling stories. My whole extended family were all storytellers, but also generous laughers, generous listeners. Particularly since my mother is a psychologist, whose favorite thing is to listen to people's feelings, I learned early on to tell stories and to delve deep.

*Why did you shift your identity, after second grade, of being a poet? Do you know?*
I decided I was going to be a senator next. I became interested in politics, and then we took a class trip to the state capital. Somebody said, "The lobbyists are the ones who really have all the power." So for a while I was going to be a lobbyist. I wasn't sure what that meant, but if they're the ones with the power, I wanted to be one of them.

I always wanted to do something important. I loved being in plays, and by high school I was directing plays at the elementary school. I performed at children's birthday parties as a clown, and I always told and wrote stories. But it didn't seem like an important thing to do. I felt like I wanted to do something, you know, hard, and important.

*Important has to be hard?*
Yes. Well, I thought so. And I also did not think that I had any talent.

I was chosen for a gifted and talented child program, when I was in fourth grade, and I tried desperately to figure out what my gift or talent was. I had heard about Mozart, how he just wrote music and had like flashes of brilliance and could just write it down and it would be perfect.

To me, a talent just came to you like that, like the first time you tried it you would be automatically brilliant at it, so I would try things.

*You didn't want to be a craftsman; you wanted to be gifted?*
Right. I dated a guy in high school who was a poet; he was very moody and clutched his hair and listened to Mahler. So I thought to be a writer you needed to be a lot moodier than I am. I've always been the least histrionic one around, and it seemed to me that to be an artist you needed to be weirder, or deeper, or moodier than I am.

I actually went to Georgetown University because I wanted to be a spy. I figured out that I had a talent and it was eavesdropping, because I have good hearing and I'm very nosy, so I'm able to hear a few conversations at once. So I decided that would be applicable to spying. I went to Georgetown to become a spy, and I was terribly bored, but it seemed like it would be important work. I was going to bring down the Berlin Wall.

*Well, that happened!*
Yes, so it may have been me, I'm not saying . . . But eventually I dropped the spying idea and I made up my own major, in English and Theater, and planned to become a playwright.

*Which you sort of are doing, by the way that you're writing.*
Right, but it's much better, because, I guess . . .

*You don't have to audition.*
Right. You don't have to audition, and when you finish the book it's done.

I started writing *Wonder* when I was working at a theater, and we were talking—I don't know why—about books for kids. Somebody was saying, "It's so ridiculous, they make it sound like, if you do the right thing then everybody will think you're great, when the truth is, no way! You do the right thing, and everybody's going to spread a rumor that you smell, or nobody's going to sit with you at lunch."

And I said, "If I ever write a book for kids (which at that point was sort of like saying if I ever get onto the Olympic bobsled team), I'll tell the truth. I would say, 'Junior high sucks!' " [This is the first line of her first book, *Wonder*.] And people laughed, which I loved.

I went home that night and I wrote it down, and then I started thinking, "That sounds like a kid. That's somebody's voice. Now whose? And what just happened to her today that made her say that?" I started writing it, not with any intention, but I was having such a good time writing it, that I decided for once in my life I was going to focus on one thing instead of trying to do everything. I quit my job at the theater and I moved home with my parents.

For the first time since I was 13 I was not making any money on my own, and my parents said, "Do it! Sit here and write this book." They had seen my plays, and they thought that this would be something that I could succeed at. I said, "I don't know if I'll ever make anything of it." And my dad said, "It won't be the first investment that I've made that went down the toilet!"

*So you had permission to fail.*
Yes.

*Which allowed you to succeed.*
Right. A friend of mine said to me, in the beginning when I was nervous, "If you never fail it means you're not trying hard enough." I try to say that to myself as often as possible.

*What has been your brick wall in writing?*
Probably that: the fear of failure, the fear that it's not good enough. A friend of mine—we were on a panel together—and he was asked, "What's your favorite book?" He said, "It's always the one that I'm working on, the one that I'm beginning right now." I was shocked, because I tend to think the one that I'm working on now is the worst of the lot, because it's not done. It's not true yet until I've done what I can do with it, and it's on its own.

My brick wall: I spend a lot of time writing in that file I told you about, that sort of journal free-form thing. "I don't even know what this character wants," and, "This is not true," and, "I don't have anything to say anyway"—that dread of the blank screen. And feeling truly the arrogance of spending my time writing down my feelings and experiences and imaginings, because, who cares?

The one main answer is, this character. I wrote *Wonder* for Jessica. She's my leader. When I know who that is, and I can write from her and for her in a truthful way, then that's when I've broken through that brick wall.

*So your internal critic is silent when you can answer, "Who is this for?" in a concrete way?*
Who is this, even more basically: who is this, what does she need, what does she want, what is she willing to go through to get it?

*Is it always your narrator that you're writing for?*
So far.

*Were you writing for* Whit*?*
Yes. You'll see after you read it [*Do-Over*] how true this is:

I got a letter from a boy who had read it. The envelope was sealed with about ten pounds of scotch tape, and he wrote, "I liked your book *Do-Over*, although I'm nothing like Whit." He went on to say, "Well, my parents split up too," and he told a few things about his life, and then wrote, "I think when Sheila dumped Whit, his heart was broken." And I thought, "Oh my God, I just got a letter from Whit!" Here's a kid who was denying every emotion he was feeling and he was feeling so deeply and so passionately. He ended it with something like, "Well, I don't know why I wrote to you anyway."

*That party at Halloween, in* Wonder, *is where* Do-Over *starts. I was wondering about that, if sometimes another book starts in the middle. Can you find a seed as you're finishing one?*
Yes, because I have questions. I wondered what happened in that closet with Sheila. What was Sheila going through? Initially, I was thinking

of a book from Sheila's point of view, but I became interested in doing something very different from *Wonder*.

Since I try to know them [the characters] so well, I feel like I could write a book from Andy's point of view, or in *Daring to Be Abigail*, some of the characters went to that camp before, the summer before *Wonder*. Well, Tracy and Nancy went to that camp the summer before that, so two years, or a year and a half before *Wonder*, in *Abigail*. I wanted to get to know Tracy better—she's so bitchy. [Laughs] She's not the main character in *Daring to Be Abigail*, but I have another book waiting someday to write from her point of view.

*Now, what was the order [of your books]?*
*Wonder* was first, and then *Do-Over*, and then *Ever After*, then *Daring to Be Abigail*. Longer and longer titles.

*And now the one about Zoe. Is this going to be an even longer title?*
[Laughs] No. Somebody pointed out to me that the first three ended in "-er," which I hadn't noticed. That's why *Daring to Be Abigail* definitely didn't want to do that; I was going to run out of "-er" words at some point.

*What is your writing routine? Your discipline?*
Well, it's become very strict. I write every morning from nine to one, a little longer if my son's nap goes well.

*You sort of answered this, but I'm going to double-check it: You had an identity as a writer when you were in second grade, and then you were not a writer, and then you were communicating more through theater and plays. One evening you just went home after the play and started writing?*
Right. But I still didn't think of myself as a writer—

*It was something you were doing because it was fun?*
I was more committed to it, and to doing it as best I could, than I had been to anything else, but I thought, "I'll try this out, sort of in between

doing theater." I guess I didn't think long-range. And in hindsight, that really helped. Many of my friends had planned on writing The Great American Novel, so that it was such a ponderous thing to begin with. I didn't have that planned.

It was only after I finished writing *Wonder* that I thought, "Well, I guess I need to figure out what to do with it now, because I spent all this time writing it." I kept thinking, "Once it's bought, I'll feel like I'm a writer." And then I thought, "Once it's published," and then I thought, "Maybe once my second one is done." And somewhere along the way, I guess, I went to a doctor's office and filled out a form, and under "Occupation," I wrote "writer." That felt like I had declared myself.

*You were literally on the record.*
Exactly. What really turned the corner for me, in being able to write, was this playwriting professor, who said, "Of course your first 20 ideas are going to be ridiculous—you've heard them already! You're going to throw those away. You need to just throw those up. Vomit those out; get past those first 20 or 40 or 50 things, just cross those out. Delete them, throw them in the garbage, and it's going to be the 51st, that might be the beginning of something worth working on."

That gave me the permission to be trite. Of course you're going to be trite 700 times, and it's not going to make any sense. It is going to be boring or stupid, so that first sentence doesn't have to be brilliant, because of course it's not going to be. You just need to get it out. And writing became less . . . exalted. And more . . . athletic.

*Athletic?*
Yes. You are getting there, and you stretch and you try, and you keep trying, and you get sweaty and dirty, and you just keep going. It is not going to come out poetry, literally, on your first effort.

*You just keep working out.*
Yes. You just keep going and going. It gave me permission not to have to be Mozart. I figured out that I had to keep making stuff up until it becomes true. It wasn't going to be true the first time I sat down.

*One of my questions is, how have you had to defend your voice? And since the voice is your directorial voice, perhaps the question is better phrased: Have you had to defend your writing?*
Yes, more often than people imagine, there are censorship questions.

There are language issues:

The first school visit I ever went on, *Wonder* had just come out. The librarian had not read it yet, and she said, "Before we start, are there any bad words in this book?" And I said, "Well, I try to choose all good words." And she said, "No, I mean, any potentially offensive words?" So I said, "Well, the first line, the first sentence is 'Junior high sucks,' and I think there may be a 'shit' in there somewhere too," and she says, "Oh my goodness, I'm new here." [Laughs]

They [my books] have been removed from shelves. I've gotten letters from teachers about content, and sexual themes, and the word "tampon" is raising some havoc with book clubs, in my fourth book.

I think that people who want to censor these kinds of things are trying to act to protect their kids. Often they have very strong opinions about premarital sex, or about language, or about nastiness among groups, or whatever their issue is.

I say to them, "This is an opportunity for you to discuss this issue with the kids in your life." If you ask the question more directly, if you ask a classroom of eighth-graders, "Have any of you gone to second?" "What do you think about touching a girl's boob?" The whole class will be under the desk. But to me it's a good way to begin a dialogue, and say, "Would you have done what Abby did in that situation? Why or why not? What do you think she should have done instead? Do you think that Mackie and Jodie have considered the risks they're taking because of their choices?"

I try to achieve some kind of honesty and some kind of verisimilitude in my writing. To do that, I need to talk about their fear of death, and their questions about sex, and use some of their language, so that it sounds like them. Other than toddlers, there's no more self-centered group of people on the planet than adolescents. So they want to read about themselves. And I want to write about them. I'm going to do it as honestly as I can.

*Was there anything that I haven't asked you that you would like to say? Have I provoked any thoughts? . . .*

*Oh yes, it's been very interesting. This morning I had an interview with author Joan Hiatt Harlow who writes for younger children. After we turned off the tape, she said, "When I finish writing something, it's like when I used to act, I have a let-down after the show, it's not exactly postpartum. My characters go off and I won't get to be with them again."*

*You keep your characters; you're like a repertory. You have this little repertoire of characters, Repertory Theater.*
Yes, it's true. There is a little bit of bittersweet to me. I think it's probably like when you put your kindergartner on the bus. You know they're coming back, and you feel proud, but you also feel like, "Oh God, let it go well!"

*Yes. Joan was speaking about hoping that her manuscript and her characters get treated well. Out in the world on their own, having kind of raised them to literary independence.*
Right. It's true.

To illuminate it, after *Do-Over* was getting some good reviews, my dad said, "It's just amazing to me that you just made up these people that I feel like I know. You just made up Whit, you made up Sheila, you made up Conor," and I said, "I didn't make up Sheila and Conor." He said, "Yes, you did. You just made them up a while ago."

Then I thought "Oh, right." To me, they weren't newly made up. I already knew them.

And that's where the beginning of the book comes in. Once I feel like they're already whole, I'm not making them up anymore. They're going about their business.

*They're formed, they're characters.*
Right. And they change. That's the fun thing with what I'm doing now: writing a series to me is being an education. I'm able to watch the characters change.

One of the realities of junior high school trauma is that if your world collapses, and you go through what is the equivalent of a divorce—your best friend breaks up with you in seventh grade on a Tuesday—you don't just have the equivalent of going to work with your newly-separated spouse, which it really is: you have to have lunch with her, and you have to sit next to her in science class because that's where your desks are now, and you have your locker next to hers, and your after-school activity is with her. Your world stays. You have to keep dealing with it. Your world is so limited.

That ongoing nature of the changing characters and their changing political scene is really interesting to me.

*There was this moment with both of my kids that reminded me of an item from a cereal box, where if you hold it one way you see one picture and if you twist it you see another. I called Matt at that age a manling, because he would go in and out of a boy to a man; you'd see the man and then the boy. It was womlet for Annie; you could just see her whole body shift. And in the next sentence they'd be little again. That's complex.*

It is. It's such a complex thing. As an adolescent, you can't keep up with yourself, whether you want to be treated like an adult or helped like a baby. You're both, or you're one or the other, and it changes so fast. It's such a complex, intense time. I don't know yet if I've achieved the honesty, the complexity of a whole person in a character, but it's my goal.

*Are you getting readers following the books and asking questions about where some of the characters went?*

Yes, kids always ask that. "So do Jessica and Conor get back together? Is it going to work out?" Molly writes in her journal, "I wish I had a best friend that I could just call up and say, 'I'm feeling so down, and so blue,' and she would say, 'hang on, I'll be right over.'" I can't tell you how many girls have quoted that passage to me because they say, "I just cry and I read this over and over again, I would be her best friend," and, "I wish I could go over because I wish she could come over to me because I feel like that right now."

"How do things turn out for her?" They all want to know that. The other wonderful thing they sometimes say is, "How did you know? I didn't think anybody knew that this happened to me! You obviously must know me!"

And then they sometimes share their stories with me. And so it continues....

# Montana Miller

*Life as an opportunity to make a good story*

**GENRE**
Nonfiction autobiography; high-risk performance and storytelling

**PUBLICATIONS INCLUDE**
*Circus Dreams: The Making of a Circus Artist* (co-author)

*Please describe your writing voice.*
When I write, I try to be honest and clear. And I don't try to put on any particular voice. So, clarity and honesty is pretty much what I go for no matter what I'm writing, which gets me in trouble a lot.

When I write for academics, I still tend to go for direct clarity. The criticism I get most often from academics is: "This is too journalistic." Because in journalism, clarity—not too wordy—makes it understandable. Get your point across. That is not what academics want. They want to sound as smart as possible, use the biggest words possible, the most convoluted constructions ...

I see my life as an opportunity to make a good story. When I write, I'm just telling what happened. That's the only reason I'm writing, really. I have done a little creative writing, but I don't consider it my strength. My creativity comes out in what I do with my life. Then, the writing part is just telling what happened.

I have bad luck trying to make up characters, very bad luck. I hope that I'll get better at this, because I would love to become a novelist, a fiction writer, someday. So far, that hasn't been my best writing, at all.

*In your story that you tell on the flying rings [a fairy tale about a princess falling in love with a lion; Montana wrote, performs, and tells the story on the rings], the medium for telling that story is your body.*
Right. And my voice.

*Yes. Is that just telling what happened?*
It is a story that came out of my experience. To me, it is not fiction. It was taking characters that symbolized what was the truth about *me*: a love affair with a lion that symbolized what was the true love affair that I had with my boyfriend. So to me, that was not a fictional character, not imagined.

That was something I lived, and then told through substituting characters—a fairy tale—the physical things about the lion. My fiancé really did remind me of a lion. And I really did grow up in the middle of the woods. Because it was something I spoke as I did physical stunts, and because of the way I performed it, it needed to be as spare as possible. There wasn't a whole lot of rich detail that I had to come up with [in words]. True, I did use other animals and fairy tale characters to tell the story, but it wasn't a story I made up. It was a story I told about me.

*How do you think fiction differs from that?*
There is not a clear line between fiction and nonfiction. In film, the line between documentary and fictional film is always really hard to draw. But it's always very clear to me that the things I write come from my own experience.

*Carolivia, in her interview, talks about how everyone is a character to her. And Megan writes creative nonfiction. There are authors who agree with you that one can't write except from experience.*

In a way, imagination is experience—if you've imagined something that's far from your own existence, and then you write about it, that's still writing from your experience, of what you imagined. I can imagine something outlandish and then go *do* it, and write about it. But I'm not very good at imagining something, not doing it, and then writing it up.

*How would you describe your genres?*

Most of the writing I do is sort of journalistic. I have one book out, *Circus Dreams*. It is romanticized autobiography. It is my story. It was co-authored. My mother and I wrote it together.

Co-authoring is a very delicate and extremely difficult thing to do. One of the reasons we were able to do it was because my mother taught me to write, she taught me everything I know. We are so close, that a lot of times, when we write something together, I can't tell who wrote what. And that's how it *should* be, ideally, for co-authors. But, in my life, also, a lot of times, it's hard for me to separate which part is her, which part is me.

I wrote most of the raw material for that book. Then we ended up deciding to change it to third person. It was a hard decision to make, and I think we should have gone the other way, because it's confusing. I think it could work both ways, but I now wish that it were in first person. Maybe just selfishly, because people look at the book and say, "Oh, your mom wrote this about you." And I say, "No, I wrote all these things." When I wrote them, it said "I," not "Montana," but people don't believe that. So, I guess it's just my own pride, that no, my mom didn't write all this! I wrote all this! And she wrote some sections, and edited it.

*What was the impetus to shifting to third person?*

We were trying to figure out what tone would sell better, what tone would grab people better. It was pretty arbitrary, there were pros and cons on both sides.

*Did you have input from your agent?*
We sold the book contract before I wrote the material, so we did have an agent. We already had an editor by the time we were getting the book out. So, yes, she must have had a lot to do with it, I don't know. I was living in France, with the circus, my mom was here discussing everything with the editor and the agent.

During that time, my main focus was, "How do I become the best trapeze artist I can, and make a career in the circus?" My mother actually proposed the book idea, got it sold, got the book contract, and said, "Okay, I'll support you, pay your rent while you are in France, and you have to earn it by writing this book."

*Was that all right with you?*
Yes, because I was writing anyway. It was good to have a reason to write. And also, because it was such a difficult world to break into, and to move into, and to adjust to.

*The circus, or publishing?*
Oh no! I had grown up in publishing! Most of the circus people grew up, not in circus families necessarily, but a lot closer to circus families than my family was. My family wasn't even athletic. I was the only athlete we'd ever had in my family. I was a gymnast. And they had never supported that at all.

So, moving from small-town Harvard, Mass., graduating from Bromfield High School, moving the next week to the middle of France where I was the only American in this circus—just a completely different world in every way—was just so hard.

So many times I wanted to give up and come home. It was really good to have this book contract keeping me there. I felt like, "Okay, say I fail at being a trapeze artist. Say I get kicked out, and I'm a complete failure, can't be a good trapeze artist. It doesn't matter, because I have a book coming out. And the year will be worth it, because this is happening."

*You were in the circus for four years.*
After the first year, it was clear that I was going to be a good trapeze artist. So after that I didn't need that safety net of having a contract to write about it.

As I grew up, we had this newspaper being published right in our home, and it's been like that since I can remember. My parents started it when I was two years old in our basement, and it's still in our basement. I've always written about everything that's happened to me. It hasn't been a job, it's just been my most effective way of communicating.

*This shifts into: What is your earliest memory of writing?*
I've been writing since before I can remember. My mom can pull out scrapbooks of stories I wrote before I even knew how to make all the letters, and you can't figure out what they're about, but, well, you can get the gist.

I learned to type when I was five, and published my own little book. We made Xeroxes. It's called "Now I Will Tell You a Story," and it's a book of stories.

I grew up in this huge house in the middle of the woods in Harvard. Ted Sizer, the education guru, was our landlord, and let us live in his summerhouse for almost nothing. My parents were dirt poor, of course, just kids out of college, and started this newspaper here in Harvard. So we lived on the top of a hill, with a mile-long dirt driveway winding around the hill. Every time there was a blizzard, we'd be snowed in, and we'd have to park the car at the bottom and walk up through the woods, with a string attached to the trees, pulling ourselves up. I grew up in this amazing house, isolated from everybody, no neighbors for miles around.

Most of my childhood I spent really believing I was an animal. Pretending so hard that I'd believe I was a horse. I spent my entire year of being seven years old insisting that I was a pony, insisting my parents introduce me as their pony, and not their daughter, and going everywhere on my hands and knees. So, I had an active imagination.

*I was going to ask, isn't this imagination?*
This is imagination, but I *lived* it! [Laughs] It wasn't like I imagined some stories about some other horses—I was it! And I, you know, lived it out! Hands and knees, holes in my jeans, everything.

*There's your body again. You proof it with your body.*
Mm-hmm. I had a cat named Shadow, which I got when I was five years old, who I loved. I fell in love with him. I married him when I was eight years old, with my father presiding, and he has been my model of unconditional love ever since. He died at age 17, when I was 22, of kidney failure, and I had his pawprint tattooed on my chest. Again, embodying, experience written on the body.

The first real stories that I typed on the typewriter and Xeroxed and published as a book were mainly about animals. My animals were characters. I've always been writing, and it seems very natural.

I was an only child till I was 6. Then my little sister came along, which was to me a big tragedy because I was so close with my parents, we were this tight triangle and they were such writers that it just seemed natural. If your parents are writers that seems like the thing to do. It didn't seem like a job. And I would never want my job to be "a writer" unless I suddenly wrote a best-seller and I had that to hold up. You can never guarantee that what you write is going to actually make you any money.

I think of writing as my most effective way of communicating. My job is more to do things that will make good stories.

That's what I think about the "how much of your identity is writer" question. To me, I'm a writer like I'm a talker. Sometimes I'll sell a piece of writing, sometimes I'll sell a piece of talking. I'll go to talk to school groups—this is actually how I make most of my money now; I'll go talk to elementary school or high school groups, do my rings act, and then talk to them for an hour about the "brave" decisions that I've made in my life to do the unexpected thing.

It depends on the school group, what I talk about. If it's a school where not many people go to college, I'm not going to talk about how they have so many options besides college. I'm going to talk about hard work, and the frustration of trying to achieve something like learning a trapeze trick that seems like you're never going to get it, and how you eventually do get it, if you stick with it.

But if it's some private school, where everyone is expected to do the standard thing, like I was—everyone expected me, as valedictorian, to go right on to Harvard and do the normal thing, and people told me I was throwing my life away—[a teacher] told me I was throwing my life away by not going to college and going to the circus instead, not believing I would ever come back and go back to school.

*How has your voice and your genre shifted over time? Do you see a shift from being a horse to being a diver?*
Not too much! Here I'm still telling a story in which I become a cat. It's actually, the creative part of that has not shifted too much. But, I'm 26, I haven't had much time to have too many shifts happen.

*You've had a very full life so far. You've done a lot.*
There's a lot to come, though. Hopefully there's a lot of shifting and growing in writing to come. Until I got to college, I really relied on this journalistic style; I always wrote for the newspaper, and the clarity of my writing was always appreciated in high school.

*Can you feel anything pulling you towards thinking about writing in different ways about different things?*
Well, I would like to write a novel about the Acapulco cliff-diving championships. My agent thinks that it would make a great novel. He asked me to write sample chapters and a plot outline, which I did, and gave to him about a month ago. It's still in the works, and I'm reluctant to keep writing until I hear "You're on the right track," or not.

It is pretty much supposed to be a trashy novel, like a subway read that would turn into a movie easily. I'm not really sure if the tone that I've struck so far is what he wants. So I'm waiting to hear on that. If he says it's good, if he sells it and I do write the rest of it, that's definitely a different tone than anything I've ever written before: "Lots of paragraphs, action tone, keep the people hooked! Make it a page-turner!" Not so much the poetic writing that I often do about diving.

*What is drawing you to your graduate school opportunities?*
I've been accepted to UCLA for the Ph.D. in Folklore.

Being in school, and being in graduate school, means a life with the flexibility and freedom to try all kinds of different things. You can take off for a year and go perform with a certain company and experience that and then write about it and analyze it for school. When you're in school you always have the freedom to try out different things and if they're failures they're *not* failures, because you still can make up something to write about them academically.

So that is what draws me to graduate school. I enjoy being a student, I enjoy the flexibility of the life. And there are not many people doing the kinds of performing I do, which is considered very high-risk, who can write about them. That is very appreciated in the academic world. High-risk performance is something that's written about by several psychologists or sociologists, but people who actually do it never write it about! Because there are so few of us.

I'm sure I'll quit, eventually, but I hope to stay in it longer to have more material because it really is fascinating to write about. To listen to some of these divers who have been in the high-diving business for 40 years, and hear the advice that they give to the rookies, it's just fascinating. The stories that are told—we're always working in crazy conditions. This is true about circus too, there are always good stories about "how we survived that show even when the lights went out and the ladder fell down and somebody broke their leg in the middle."

*There's a special bonding, community ties through surviving that too.*
Oh, absolutely. I haven't been in the business of high-diving too long, but I think that you do learn who is truly your friend and who's not. Just by knowing the people long enough and watching their behavior long enough.

*Have you had to defend your writing voice, and your choice of how you talk? You spoke about having to defend it to your [senior thesis] committee.* That's the main time I've had to defend it in that sense, yes. The academics, the professors saying, "This is not academic enough. This is too journalistic." And in a way, they have a point sometimes. When they say it's too journalistic, sometimes they mean it stays too much on the surface of what happened, and doesn't go deep enough into analysis. And so, in that sense, I know they're right.

I hope that in graduate school I'll learn better how to do analysis in a way that's true enough so that I'm still clear, and I am saying things that have basis. In academics you have to back up your points really thoroughly, and sometimes, if you don't have a firm enough grasp of the subject, it's easy to try to back up your points using famous people's writing, or using other people's theories without really . . . Well, just because they sound good on the surface, and they sort of sound like they back up your point, but without really knowing there is a connection there.

The other thing that comes to mind when you say, "How have you had to defend your voice," is my mother's writing and my writing, and my mother's life and my life. She had me when she was 19, and we've always had an extremely close bond. We're very psychic with each other. Whenever I'm having trouble writing something—I never get exactly blocked, but a lot of times I have a lot of trouble getting the tone right, especially when I'm first starting out something, or making something clear.

She's always been my writing coach. And she's always been my hero. I can't tell you how much I love my mother, and how much I admire her, and model myself on her. She's such a smart and strong woman, that why wouldn't I want to imitate her and let her help me when I'm struggling?

And a lot of times the result is that I'm not really sure whose work it is. When we co-authored a book, that was okay, because that's the goal when you co-author, is that you mesh so well that you're not really sure whose writing it is. You don't want to have a book that's co-authored where you can see, "Oh, that's where so-and-so started to write," and where there's a clear division.

But, when it's important—and sometimes it is very important—for me to write something that is mine, because she is available to me, and willing, and I enjoy working with her so much, and I know that it's helpful to the quality of my writing, then I have to be careful about defending what is my work against . . .

It feels strange to say, because I'm not talking about defending my writing—it's like, I'm opening my arms to the thing I should be defending against. It doesn't feel like an attack. But in some ways, I know it's destructive to my own growth as a writer and as a person. And I have to force myself to separate from my mother in a lot of ways.

*What role has silence played in your writing?*
I've thought about that question, trying to figure out what I would answer to that, and I keep coming up with nothing.

*Have you ever been silenced in your writing?*
I've been talking about my mother and me. When I'm at a loss for words, my mother will speak for me. If she were not here, I will think of what she would say and say that. So, in that sense, I've never really felt that I was silenced, because either she was here to speak for me, or I could think to myself, "Okay, what would she tell me to do, or do, if she were in this trouble that I'm in?"

At the times when I've needed the most courage, like to fight a newspaper advisor who was trying to censor me, or to interview with some *New York Times* person that I was really intimidated by, she's my inspiration, my model, and I draw my courage and my ideas and my behavior from her. So, in that way, no, I've never found myself having to be silent. But because I am taking that from her, in some way, yes, she takes over in me.

Silence is the part that is purely Montana, the part that, when I was seven, if somebody came to our house, I would hide under the table and they couldn't get me out. And that's definitely a silent Montana who *wants* to be silent.

In many ways, I want to be silent, and I'm forced by my upbringing, and by the pressures that are on me, not to be.

*I knew you in high school as very quiet. And so when I heard you were writing a book I was delighted, because I knew there would be more words coming out of you. Whenever I saw you, you were always very quiet taking things in, through every pore, quiet but not invisible.*
  *One of the things that silence can do is get people in touch with what's happening in their body, and you're so in touch with that.*
  *For myself, for instance, in order to get in touch with what other information I'm taking in, a gut instinct, an intuitive flash, a heartfelt feeling, words stuck in my throat, I need to move to silence, to let my body speak. You seem to have a constant dialogue. You have broadband connections between your head and your body. You've worked so much with both that you do not need to move to silence, for hunches or memories or feelings to come through.*
Maybe you're right. I think it would be good for me to learn how to do the silence thing. I'm terrible at meditation, I can't do yoga, and I'm not very skilled at this calm, silent—

*Yet, when I looked at you standing on those cliffs [for diving], you were totally still, and poised and focused, and when you go to leap off—*
Maybe those are the brief moments of silence that I do manage to capture. Maybe that's one of the things I like about cliff diving and high diving. When you are up there and you are about to do the thing, you *have* to focus in a sort of meditative way. It doesn't last very long, but you cannot be observing yourself from without. You can't be thinking what you're going to write about it. You have to be completely there.

*What animal went under the table when somebody would come to the house when you were 7?*
Usually a cat, or a horse—I guess a horse would have a harder time hiding, wouldn't it? The elephant in the room, so to speak! [Laughs] Cat. Rabbits, too.

My favorite book ever is *Watership Down*. Also my favorite movie. When I read that, I think I was about eight or nine. I got sort of a sense of religion. My mom was raised Catholic and my dad is what you might call an agnostic Jew, and we always celebrated *all* the different holidays, for the sake of celebration. We would tell the Chanukah story and . . . then we would tell the Easter story . . . and then we'd do Passover. I was raised with a belief that there is some kind of God, but also an awareness that everybody thinks of it in a different way, and who knows what's true?

When I read the Narnia books, I decided that Aslan was God. The big lion. Then, when I read *Watership Down,* I loved the rabbits' conception of God, Frith, the sun, and El Erairah, the rabbit hero. My main religious influences for me personally, as far as real spirituality goes, were animals. I've always really identified with rabbits, but I enjoy cats more because they purr, and curl up with you.

*What has been your brick wall, your nemesis in writing?*
I think it's too early in my life to [know] that. So far, the walls that I've run up against, like, "This isn't quite what we want; no, we're rejecting this. No, we don't want to publish that," have been, I think, when I hear other writers talk, the things that every writer goes through before they become successful.

*Those sound like external walls.*
Yes. They are external walls. Yes. Those are the only walls I come up against in writing. As I said, to me I'm a writer like I'm a talker.

*Is there anything else not asked that you would like to say?*
I would like to emphasize that idea of my parents teaching me as they coached me in writing: the best stories are often stories about failure, fear, struggle, humiliation. Knowing that so deeply has been a real safety net for me in trying some experiences that are terrifying and that I think there's a good chance I'll fail at.

Like becoming a trapeze artist or going down to Acapulco to dive from the cliffs. Or any kind of scary thing that I try, I get the courage from that by knowing it's okay if I fail because failure makes the best stories.

Even though my parents ... didn't want me to go to Acapulco. They never wanted me to devote my life to acrobatics, but they do have a true sense of the value of story.

The downside of that is when, in my life, I'm *not* doing something that makes a good story—when all I'm doing is being a student, going to class, or working, when I have a safe and normal existence, which doesn't make such a good story. I hope that someday I'll be a good enough writer to make good stories out of more normal kinds of existence, because I do read wonderful novels about people who are having much more normal lives than I am! But when I'm in those periods of my life, I have a sense of being worthless. Like, in order to be valuable and worthwhile, I have to be doing something that grabs people and pulls them in to a compelling, page-turner story. That is so important to me that I'm almost incapable of turning down offers like "Want to go to Acapulco and dive from an 80-foot cliff?" And that feels really dangerous and tragic to me.

So maybe one of my goals as a writer is to learn how to tell stories in a compelling way that doesn't have to be about such death-defying situations.

*You know as an athlete the importance of taking a day off. And those are silences in the physical routine. It is important to have the silences or quiet times in life, to refuel.*

Those times, even though I know that I need them, and my body often forces me to take them—I'll get injured or I'll just get too tired and have to stop diving and do nothing for a while—during those times, I start to feel extremely depressed.... At those times, it rushes in and is often so overwhelming to me. I've never been suicidal, and would never even consider committing suicide—its not like that. I've always come through depression, and I've always been sure that I *would* come through. But it always is more of a risk that I'll fall into depression when I'm not doing something, when I'm not performing, in a high-diving show, or in a trapeze act.

I need that external applause, whether it's applause for my writing or applause for my physical exploits, and I hope that someday I won't need it so much. Because it's going to be exhausting to have a life where I have to constantly be doing this stuff. It's very exhausting and dangerous.

# APPENDIX ONE

# Selected Books by Authors Interviewed

[In alphabetical order]

### REGINA BARRECA

www.ginabarreca.com

*Too Much of a Good Thing is Wonderful.* Storrs, Conn.: Bibliopola Press, 2000. Humorous essays about events in Barreca's life.

*The Signet Book of American Humor* (editor). New York: Signet Classics, 1999. Explores the American humor tradition from the 1700s to present.

*The Erotics of Instruction* (editor). Hanover, N.H.: University Press of New England, 1997. Essays explore the dynamics that shape teaching and the exchange of knowledge.

*The Penguin Book of Women's Humor* (editor). New York: Penguin Books, 1996. Explores women's unique sense of humor, from 1500 to the present.

*New Perspectives on Women and Comedy: Studies in Gender and Culture,* Vol. 5 (editor). Philadelphia: Gordon & Breach, 1996. Twenty-one original essays exploring how women use humor to break down cultural stereotypes.

*Sweet Revenge: The Wicked Delights of Getting Even.* New York: Harmony Books, 1995. Explores the themes and dynamics of revenge in literature and contemporary culture. Translated into German and Chinese.

*Desire and Imagination: Classic Essays in Sexuality* (editor). New York: Meridian, 1995. Essays on human sexuality, from 1812 to 1920.

*Untamed and Unabashed: Essays on Women and Humor in British Literature (Humor in Life and Letters)*. Detroit: Wayne State University Press, 1994. Explores the use of humor in British authors from Austen to Fay Weldon.

*Fay Weldon's Wicked Fictions* (editor). Hanover, N.H.: University Press of New England, 1994. Essays examining Weldon's literature.

*Perfect Husbands (& Other Fairy Tales): Demystifying Marriage, Men, and Romance.* New York: Harmony Books, 1993. Looks at the changing role and image of the husband in American popular culture and literature since 1900. Translated into Swedish and Chinese.

*They Used to Call Me Snow White . . . But I Drifted: Women's Strategic Use of Humor.* New York: Viking, 1991. Examines women's humor in popular culture, theater, literature, and everyday life.

*Sex and Death in Victorian Literature* (editor). Bloomington: Indiana University Press, 1990. Essays on 19th-century literature.

## CAROLINE BIRD

*Lives of Our Own: Secrets of Salty Old Women.* Boston: Houghton Mifflin, 1995. Stories of single women over 55 showing how they can live healthy, independent lives and develop their full potential and a positive self-image.

*Second Careers: New Ways to Work after Fifty.* New York: Little, Brown & Co., 1992. Based on experiences of 6,000 working seniors in second careers.

*The Two-Paycheck Marriage: How Women at Work Are Changing Life in America.* New York: Rawson, Wade Publishers, 1979. Documents how women's entrance into the working world has changed family, marriage, the workplace, and society.

*Everything a Woman Needs to Know to Get Paid What She's Worth.* New York: David McKay Co., 1973. Information and advice to working women on careers, volunteer work, and receiving the pay they deserve.

*The Crowding Syndrome: Learning to Live with Too Much and Too Many.* New York: David McKay Co., 1972. Tackles concerns of overpopulation and economic growth.

*Born Female: The High Cost of Keeping Women Down.* New York: David McKay Co., 1968. Addresses women's roles in society and points to the social and economic disadvantages of "keeping women down."

*The Invisible Scar.* New York: David McKay Co., 1966. Examines the Great Depression and its effect on America.

## JOAN HIATT HARLOW

www.joanhiattharlow.com

*Joshua's Song.* New York: Margaret K. McElderry Books, 2001. During the influenza epidemic of 1918, a 13-year-old Bostonian newspaper boy finds himself close to an explosion that sends tons of molasses through the streets.

*Star in the Storm.* New York: Margaret K. McElderry Books, 2000. In this middle-grade novel, a 12-year-old Newfoundland girl keeps her dog hidden after a new law in her village bans all non-sheepherding dogs. Winner of the ASPCA Henry Bergh Children's Book Award for Humane Fiction.

*Shadow Bear.* New York: Doubleday, 1981. Picture book, in which an Eskimo child and a polar bear discover each other's shadows. Translated into German, Swedish, and Danish.

*The Dark Side of the Creek.* Wright Group/McGraw-Hill, 2000. An environmental mystery chapter-book.

*The Creatures of Sand Castle Key.* Wright Group/McGraw-Hill, 2001. A sequel to *The Dark Side of the Creek.*

## CAROLIVIA HERRON

www.carolivia.org

*Nappy Hair.* New York: Knopf, 1997. Picture book for young readers, using a call-and-response narrative style, in which various people at a backyard picnic offer comments on a young girl's tightly curled "nappy hair."

*Selected Works of Angelina Weld Grimke* (editor). Oxford: Oxford University Press, 1991. Volume presents the major works of Angelina Weld Grimke, abolitionist and women's rights advocate, written between 1905-1920.

*Thereafter Johnnie.* New York: Random House, 1991. Epic adult novel that follows the turmoil of an African-American family in Washington, D.C. "Luminous and visionary." —*Los Angeles Times Book Review.*

## MEGAN LEBOUTILLIER

*"No" Is a Complete Sentence: Learning the Sacredness of Personal Boundaries.* New York: Ballantine Books, 1995. Self-help book offers ways to establish and maintain healthy personal boundaries and develop behaviors to create more freedom and self-awareness.

*Little Miss Perfect.* MAC Publishing, 1987. Self-help book offering strategies for children growing up dealing with alcoholism in their family.

## MONTANA MILLER

www.montanamiller.com

*Circus Dreams: The Making of a Circus Artist.* Boston: Joy Street Books, 1990. Text and photographs follow the journey of 18-year-old Montana Miller as she attends the National Center for the Circus Arts in France to pursue her dream of becoming a trapeze artist. Co-authored with Kathleen Cushman.

## PHYLLIS HOGE THOMPSON

Hawai'i Award for Literature 1995

*The Painted Clock: Mogollon in the '80s.* The Wildflower Press, 2002. Non-fiction. A newly married couple discover, as they face one another's foibles, the demands and surprises of living among ghost-town eccentrics.

*Letters from Jian Hui and Other Poems.* The Wildflower Press, 2001. Poems based on real letters from a young Chinese woman struggling to find a good life in Beijing.

*A Field of Poetry.* Japan, 2000. Translations by Hideo Yokokawa into Japanese of poems selected from previous volumes.

*The Ghosts of Who We Were.* Urbana, Ill.: University of Illinois Press, 1986. Themes of separation by time and distance called up by ghosts of life past and recollection of places.

*What the Land Gave.* Quarterly Review of Literature, Poetry Series III, 1981. QRL Poetry Series Award poems: reflections on landscapes, responses to dissolving relationships, and contemporary expressions of classical mythology.

*The Serpent of the White Rose.* Honolulu: Petronium Press, 1973. Block-print-illustrated retelling in rhymed stanzas of the Norse folk-tale "Prince Lindworm."

*The Creation Frame.* Urbana, Ill.: University of Illinois Press, 1973. Poems in response to nature, place, and the arts, particularly painting.

*Artichoke and Other Poems.* Honolulu: University of Hawai'i Press, 1969. Early poems often Hawaiian in situation and milieu.

## RACHEL VAIL

*Sometimes I'm Bombaloo.* New York: Scholastic, 2001. When Kate feels angry and out of control, her mother helps her to be herself again. Picture book for ages 3-7.

*Fill in the Blank (The Friendship Ring Series).* New York: Scholastic, 2000. Tommy falls in love with Zoe.

*Popularity Contest (The Friendship Ring Series).* New York: Scholastic, 2000. Seventh-grader Zoe runs for class president and tries to win the approval of her classmates.

*What Are Friends For? (The Friendship Ring Series).* New York: Scholastic, 1999. Olivia learns that she must always speak up for herself, regardless of what her friends think of her.

*Over the Moon.* New York: Orchard Books, 1998. Picture book for children ages 3-7 in which a cow tries to jump over the moon.

*Not That I Care (The Friendship Ring Series).* New York: Scholastic, 1998. Seventh-grader Morgan Miller must choose ten items to present to her class that represent who she is.

*Please, Please, Please (The Friendship Ring Series).* New York: Scholastic, 1998. CJ, a talented ballerina, struggles with her conflicting desires to study ballet and please her mother, or to quit and be like the other kids at school.

*If You Only Knew (The Friendship Ring Series).* New York: Scholastic, 1998. Seventh-grader Zoe comes from a big family and seeks a friendship with CJ.

*Daring to Be Abigail: A Novel.* New York: Puffin, 1996. Eleven-year-old Abby deals with the pains of adolescence and the loss of her father while at summer camp.

*Ever After.* New York: Orchard Books, 1994. Fourteen-year-old Molly seeks her own identity while learning about the complexities of friendship.

*Do-Over.* New York: Orchard Books, 1992. Thirteen-year-old Whitman must deal with his feelings towards his father, his parents' separation, and the excitement of acting in his first play.

*Wonder.* New York: Orchard Books, 1991. Everything changes for 12-year-old Jessica when she enters junior high and is no longer part of the "in" crowd.

## YOKO KAWASHIMA WATKINS

*My Brother, My Sister and I.* New York: Simon & Schuster Books for Young Readers, 1994. Living as impoverished refugees in 1947 Japan, 13-year-old Yoko and her siblings endure many struggles while in search of their missing father. An ALA Best Book for Young Adults; *New York Times* Notable Book.

*Tales from the Bamboo Grove.* New York: Bradbury Press, 1992. Six Japanese folk tales, along with poignant recollections from her childhood days of how the tales were told in her own family's tradition.

*So Far from the Bamboo Grove.* New York: Lothrop, Lee, & Shepard, 1986. Fictionalized autobiography that tells how 11-year-old Yoko escaped from northern Korea to Japan with her mother and sister at the end of WWII. An ALA Notable Book.

## LOUISE M. WISECHILD

*The Mother I Carry: A Memoir of Healing from Emotional Abuse.* Seattle: Seal Press, 1993. An eloquent, moving exploration of the author's relationship with her emotionally abusive mother, tracing a path to wholeness.

*She Who Was Lost Is Remembered: Healing from Incest Through Creativity* (editor). Seattle: Seal Press, 1991. Anthology presents the work and personal essays of women artists, writers, and musicians who used their artistic skills and creativity to heal from childhood abuse.

*The Obsidian Mirror: An Adult Healing from Incest.* Seattle: Seal Press, 1988. Discusses the author's personal recovery from childhood abuse and incest. "A singular literary achievement." —*Publishers Weekly.*

# APPENDIX TWO

# *Bibliography of Reference Works*

Bateson, Mary Catherine. *Composing a Life.* New York: Penguin, 1990.

Behar, Ruth. *Translated Woman: Crossing the Border with Esperanza's Story.* Boston: Beacon Press, 1993.

Belenky, Mary Field, Blythe McVicker Clinchy, Nancy Rule Goldberger, Jill Marruck Tarule. *Women's Ways of Knowing: The Development of Self, Voice, and Mind.* New York: Basic Books, 1986.

Berry, Cicely. *Voice and the Actor.* New York: Macmillan, 1973.

Bettelheim, Bruno. *The Uses of Enchantment: The Meaning and Importance of Fairy Tales.* New York: Vintage Books, Random House, 1977.

Boleslavsky, Richard. *Acting: The First Six Lessons.* New York: Theatre Arts Books, 1933.

Castillejo, Irene Claremont. *Knowing Woman: A Feminine Psychology.* New York: Harper & Row, 1973.

Cheever, Susan. *A Woman's Life: The Story of an Ordinary American and Her Extraordinary Generation.* New York: William Morrow and Company, Inc., 1994.

Cheng, Nien. "From Life and Death in Shanghai." In *The Norton Book of Women's Lives,* ed. by Phyllis Rose. New York: W. W. Norton, 1993.

Clark, J. Milton, and Carol Peterson Haviland. "Language and Authority: Shifting the Privilege." *Journal of Basic Writing,* 1995.

Connelly, F. Michael, and D. Jean Clandinin. "Stories of Experience and Narrative Inquiry." *Educational Researcher,* June-July, 1990.

Conway, Jill Ker, ed. *Written by Herself: Autobiographies of American Women, an Anthology.* New York: Random House, 1992.

Cormier, Robert. *I Have Words to Spend: Reflections of a Small-Town Editor.* Edited by Constance Senay Cormier. New York: Delacorte Press, Bantam Doubleday Bell Publishing Group, 1991.

Crowley-Long, Kathleen, and Kenneth J. Long. "Searching for Models of Fully Functioning Women." *Women and Therapy,* special issue: *Finding Voice: Writing by New Authors,* 1992.

Dickerson, Mary Jane. "A Voice of One's Own: Creating Writing Identities." Paper presented at the 39th Conference on College Composition and Communication, St. Louis, Mo., March 17-19, 1988.

Elbow, Peter. *Writing Without Teachers.* New York: Oxford University Press, 1973.

Estes, Clarissa Pinkola. "Clear Water: Nourishing the Creative Life." In *Women Who Run with the Wolves: Myths and Stories of the Wild Woman Archetype.* New York: Ballantine Books, 1992.

Freire, Paulo. *Pedagogy of the Oppressed.* New York: Continuum, 1993.

Friday, Nancy. *The Power of Beauty.* New York: HarperCollins, 1996.

Friedland, Ellie. "Look and Look Again: A Heuristic Inquiry into Education as Awareness." Doctoral thesis, Union Institute & University, 1994.

Fromm, Erich. *The Forgotten Language: An Introduction to the Understanding of Dreams, Fairy Tales, and Myths.* New York: Grove Press, 1952.

Gardner, Howard. *Frames of Mind: The Theory of Multiple Intelligences.* New York: Basic Books, 1993.

_____. *Leading Minds: An Anatomy of Leadership.* New York: Basic Books, 1996.

Gilligan, Carol. *In a Different Voice: Psychological Theory and Women's Development.* Cambridge, Mass.: Harvard University Press, 1982.

_____, Nona P. Lyons, and Trudy J. Hanmer, eds. *Making Connections: The Relational Worlds of Adolescent Girls at Emma Willard School.* Cambridge, Mass.: Harvard University Press, 1989.

Gluck, Sherna Berger, and Daphne Patai. *Women's Words: The Feminist Practice of Oral History.* New York: Routledge, 1991.

Greenberg, Jay R. and Stephen A. Mitchell. *Object Relations in Psychoanalytic Theory.* Cambridge, Mass.: Harvard University Press, 1983.

Grow, Gerald. "Writing and the Seven Intelligences." Tallahassee, Fla.: Florida A&M University, 1995.

Hardymon, Betsy L. "A Mother Re-Envisions Her Daughter's Writing." *Journal of Teaching Writing,* 10.2 (Fall/Winter 1991): 137-50.

Heilbrun, Carolyn G. *Writing a Woman's Life.* New York: Ballantine Books, 1988.

Hirschfield, Jane, ed. *Women in Praise of the Sacred: 43 Centuries of Spiritual Poetry by Women.* New York: Harper Collins, 1994.

Howe, Florence, ed. *No More Masks! An Anthology of Twentieth-Century American Women Poets.* New York: Harper Collins, 1993.

Huckvale, Mark. "Illustrating Speech: Analogies Between Speaking and Writing." *Speech, Hearing and Language,* 1992.

Hurwitt, Annika. "Mending the Broken Cord: Using Stories With Women Survivors of Sexual Abuse." Doctoral thesis, Union Institute & University, 1993.

*Intimate Environments: Sex, Intimacy, and Gender in Families.* Edited by David Kantor and Barbara F. Oken. New York: The Guilford Press, Guilford Publications, 1989.

Jung, Carl Gustav. *Memories, Dreams, Reflections.* Translated by Richard and Clara Winston. Edited by Aniela Jaffe. Revised ed. New York: Vintage Books, Random House, 1961.

Kaplan, Louise J. *No Voice is Ever Wholly Lost.* New York: Simon & Schuster, 1995.

Kegan, Robert, and Lisa Laskow Lahey. *How the Way We Talk Can Change the Way We Work: Seven Languages for Transformation.* San Francisco: Jossey-Bass, 2000.

Keithley, Zoe. "My Own Voice: Students Say It Unlocks the Writing Process." *Journal of Basic Writing,* Fall 1992.

Kernberg, Otto. *Object Relations Theory and Clinical Psychoanalysis.* New York: Jason Aronson, 1976.

Klein, Melanie. *Envy and Gratitude & Other Works, 1946-1963.* New York: Dell, 1975.

Lamott, Anne. *Bird by Bird: Some Instructions on Writing and Life.* New York: Anchor Books, Doubleday, 1994.

Landy, David. *Culture, Disease, and Healing: Studies in Medical Anthropology.* New York: Macmillan, 1977.

Lee, John with Ceci Miller-Kritsberg. *Writing from the Body: For Writers, Artists, and Dreamers Who Long to Free Your Voice.* New York: St. Martin's Press, 1994.

Leonard, Linda Schierse. *The Wounded Woman: Healing the Father-Daughter Relationship.* Boulder, Colo.: Shambhala, 1983.

McKeegan, Patricia. "Only She Who Attempts the Absurd Can Achieve the Impossible: Rethinking the Dream." *Women and Therapy,* special issue: *Finding Voice: Writing by New Authors,* 1992.

McLean Taylor, Jill, and Carol Gilligan, and Amy M. Sullivan. *Between Voice and Silence: Women and Girls, Race and Relationship.* Cambridge, Mass.: Harvard University Press, 1997.

Morrison, Toni. *Beloved.* New York: Penguin Books, 1987.

Moustakas, Clark. *Heuristic Research: Design, Methodology, and Applications.* Newbury Park, Calif.: Sage Publications, 1990.

Noble, Vicki. *Shakti Woman: Feeling Our Fire, Healing Our World, the New Female Shamanism.* San Francisco: HarperCollins, 1991.

Novak, Elaine Adams. *Styles of Acting: A Scenebook for Aspiring Actors.* Englewood Cliffs, N.J.: Prentice Hall, 1985.

O'Leary, Maureen E. "A Voice of One's Own: Born, Achieved, or Thrust Upon One?" Paper presented at the 44th Annual Conference on College Composition and Communication, San Diego, Calif., March 31-April 3, 1993.

Olsen, Tillie. *Silences: Classic Essays on the Art of Creating.* New York: Delta/Seymour Lawrence, 1965.

Patai, Daphne. "U.S. Academics and Third World Women: Is Ethical Research Possible?" In *Women's Words: The Feminist Practice of Oral History,* edited by Sherna Berger Gluck and Daphne Patai. New York: Routledge, 1991.

Pearlman, Mickey. *Listen to Their Voices: 20 Interviews with Women Who Write.* Boston: Houghton Mifflin, 1993.

Reik, Theodor. *Listening with the Third Ear.* New York: Farrar, Straus and Company, 1948.

Richardson, Laurel. *Writing Strategies: Reaching Diverse Audiences.* Vol. 21, ed. Newbury Park, Calif.: Sage Publications, 1990.

Rogers, Annie G. *A Shining Affliction: A Story of Harm and Healing in Psychotherapy.* New York: Viking Penguin, 1995.

Rose, Mike. *Lives on the Boundary.* New York: Penguin Books, 1989.

Rountree, Cathleen. *On Women Turning 50: Celebrating Mid-Life Discoveries.* San Francisco: HarperCollins, 1991.

Ruddick, Sara, and Pamela Daniels, eds. *Working It Out: 23 Women Writers, Artists, Scientists, and Scholars Talk About Their Lives and Work.* New York: Pantheon Books, 1977.

Sapphire. *American Dreams.* New York: Vintage, 1996.

———. *Push.* New York: Knopf, 1996.

Schapira, Laurie Layton. *The Cassandra Complex: Living with Disbelief.* Toronto: Inner City Books, 1988.

Stiles, Claudia Gafford. "The Myriad Forms of Magic: A Narrative on Poetry and Grief." *Journal of Poetry Therapy,* Vol. 8, no. 3, Spring 1995.

Sullivan, Harry Stack. *The Interpersonal Theory of Psychiatry.* Edited by Helen Swick Perry and Mary Ladd Gawel. New York: W. W. Norton & Company, 1953.

Tannen, Deborah. *Gender and Discourse.* New York: Oxford University Press, 1994.

Tobey, Linda. *The Integrity Moment: Making Powerful Choices in Life.* Dubuque, Iowa: Kendall-Hunt Publishing Company, 2001.

Welty, Eduora. *One Writer's Beginnings.* New York: Warner Books, 1983.

Woolf, Virginia. *A Writer's Diary.* Edited by Leonard Woolf. Harcourt Brace. New York, 1954.

*Women in Ritual and Symbolic Roles.* Edited by Judith and Anita Spring Hoch-Smith. New York: Plenum Press, 1978.

# APPENDIX THREE

## *Credits*

p. 15: Original architectural drawing of a doorway, © Raphael Architects, Michael Raphael, Principal. www.raphaelarchitects.com. Reprinted with permission. All rights reserved.

p 17: Doorway, photograph. © Terry Barnum. PC Barnum Photography. Reprinted with permission. All rights reserved. Taken at Fruitlands Museum, Harvard, Mass., the home where Louisa May Alcott lived and about which she later wrote in her book *Transcendental Wild Oats*.

p. 26 and p. 35: Dr. Jean Shinoda Bolen is quoted from her interview in Cathleen Rountree's book *On Women Turning 50: Celebrating Mid-Life Discoveries*, p. 212. Published by HarperSanFrancisco, 1993. © Cathleen Rountree.

p. 27: Clare Goodwin created the crow mandala especially for this book. © B. Clare Goodwin, 2002. Reprinted with permission. All rights reserved. For additional artwork, see www.abgoodwin.com/mandala.

p. 29: Quoted passage is from an article by Betsy L. Hardymon, "A Mother Re-Envisions Her Daughter's Writing," published in the *Journal of Teaching Writing*, 10.2 (Fall/Winter 1991): pp. 137-50. Hardymon is referencing work by Donald Graves and Virginia Stuart.

p. 32: Quoted passage is reprinted by permission of the publisher, from *In a Different Voice: Psychological Theory and Women's Development*, by Carol Gilligan, Cambridge, Mass.: Harvard University Press, Copyright © 1982, 1993 by Carol Gilligan.

p. 32-33: Quoted passage is from the University Sermon at the Memorial Church of Harvard University, Cambridge, Mass., preached April 13, 1997, by The Right Reverend and Right Honourable Lord Runcie of Cuddesdon, 102nd Archbishop of Canterbury and High Steward of the University of Cambridge, Cambridge, England.

p. 47: The concept and design of this illustration are attributed to Leland Bradford. Bradford was the founder of T-groups in the 1950s and worked for the National Training Laboratories.

p. 56: Quoted passage is from Theodor Reik's *Listening with the Third Ear.* New York: Farrar, Straus and Company, 1948, p. 144

p. 57: Quoted passage is from an interview Jill Hackett conducted with author Robert Cormier on April 18, 1997, in Fitchburg, Mass.

p. 59 and pp. 132-134: Phyllis Hoge Thompson reads here from a piece she wrote which was published in the book *What the Land Gave,* Vol. XXII of the Quarterly Review of Literature Poetry Book Series. Reprinted with permission.

p. 60-61: Poem and rough draft © Phyllis Hoge Thompson. Reprinted with permission. All rights reserved.

p. 69: Artwork (titled "Africa: Love-Magic") © Betty LaDuke. Reprinted with permission. All rights reserved. For more of her work, see website at www.BettyLaDuke.com.

p. 70: Howard Gardner quotes are from his book *Leading Minds: An Anatomy of Leadership.* New York: Basic Books, 1993.

p. 80: Quoted passage is copyright © Jacquelyn Mitchard, from her syndicated column *The Rest of Us.* This article, titled "For women writers, quiet time is golden," appeared in *The Sun,* Chicago (Sunday, April 10, 1997), pp. A1, A4. www.previewport.com/Home/mitchard.html.

p. 91: The study referenced is described by Dr. Julie White in her audiocassette program *Image & Self-Projection: For Today's Woman in Business, Government and the Professions* (Boulder, Colo.: Career/Track Publications, 1984).

p. 93: Cartoon © Marian Henley, from *Maxine! Comix* by Marian Henley. Reprinted by permission of the artist. For more of her work, see website at www.Maxine.net.

p. 94: Quoted passage is from Richard Boleslavsky's *Acting: The First Six Lessons.* New York: Theatre Arts Books, 1933.

p. 126: The photo of author Yoko Kawashima Watkins is by Paul Harder.

p. 174: The photo of author Jill Hackett is by Matt Fifield.

p. 196: Passage quoted by Regina Barreca is from Rita Mae Brown's book *Southern Discomfort,* published by Harper & Row, 1992.

# APPENDIX FOUR

## Index of Authors' Themes

These entries are here for you to dip into the interviews on subjects that interest you. Entry locations are authors' initials and page numbers.

Regina Barreca (RB)
Caroline Bird (CB)
Jill Hackett (JH)
Joan Hiatt Harlow (JHH)
Carolivia Herron (CH)
Megan LeBoutillier (ML)
Montana Miller (MM)
Phyllis Hoge Thompson (PHT)
Rachel Vail (RV)
Yoko Kawashima Watkins (YKW)
Louise Wisechild (LW)

Audience. RB: 188, 189, 194, 197; CB: 101-102; JHH: 141; CH: 154; ML: 200; RV: 214, 224, 229-230; YKW: 115; LW: 177, 181

Brother. RB: 193; CH: 157; ML: 201; YKW: 114, 117, 120, 121, 123

Characters, creating. JHH: 145, 146; CH: 159; ML: 204; MM: 232; RV: 213-216, 225, 228

Community, connection to. RB: 197; JH: 168; CH: 153-154, 162; YKW: 125; LW: 177, 186

Creative wound. ML: 201, 203

Critics, internal and external. RB: 195; CB: 102-103; CH: 155, 162-163; ML: 201; RV: 228; YKW: 122; LW: 178, 180, 182-183

Defending voice. RB: 189, 194; CB: 102-103; JH: 169-170, 173; CH: 159, 162-163; ML: 200-201; MM: 239; PHT: 129; RV: 227; YKW: 116-121; LW: 175-176, 178-179

Dream of being a writer. CB: 102; CH: 157; ML: 200; LW: 177-178

Education, elementary. JH: 168; JHH: 142, 146; CH: 153, 154, 161, 166; ML: 201; PHT: 129-130, 132; RV: 220; YKW: 116-121; LW: 178

Education, higher. RB: 188-189, 190, 191-192; CB: 108; JH: 170, 173; CH: 159, 160; ML: 200, 204, 207, 209; MM: 238, 239; PHT: 130, 132-133; RV: 218, 222; LW: 178, 184

Education, jr/sr high school.; CB: 108; JH: 170; JHH: 143-144; ML: 202, 211; RV: 218, 221, 227, 229

Education, middle. YKW: 115

Father. RB: 188; CB: 108, 109; JH: 168, 173; JHH: 143; CH: 165; ML: 210; MM: 242; RV: 219, 220, 221, 223, 228; YKW: 118-121, 122; LW: 181

Fear. RB: 194; JHH: 140, 144; ML: 202; LW: 177, 181

Genre. CB: 103; JHH: 142, 146; CH: 153, 154-155, 158, 159, 160-161; ML: 202-203; MM: 232, 233; PHT: 129, 130; RV: 217; YKW: 115

Hiatus from writing. CH: 158; JH: 169-170, 171; ML: 201, 204, 210; YKW: 123

Humor. RB: 190-191, 192, 193, 194

Ignored, being. ML: 201, 202, 210-211; YKW: 122; LW: 180

Imagination. JHH: 149; CH: 156, 159; MM: 233, 235-236; YKW: 125-126

Intelligence. RB: 188-189; JH: 171

Journaling. ML: 199, 200, 210; RV: 223; LW: 184

Language. RB: 189-190, 191, 194; CB: 106-107; JHH: 143; CH: 154-155, 165-166; PHT: 128, 129, 131, 132, 133; RV: 227; YKW: 113-114, 115, 126

Memory, earliest of writing. RB: 193; CB: 108; JH: 168; JHH: 142; CH: 156-157; ML: 200-201, 209; MM: 235, 236; PHT: 131; RV: 218-219, 220; YKW: 126

Mother. RB: 188, 192; JH: 168, 173; JHH: 146, 147; CH: 156, 157, 165; ML: 200, 201, 204; MM: 233, 239-240, 242; PHT: 129, 132, ; RV: 214, 215, 219, 220, 221, 223; YKW: 116, 117, 118, 119-120, 122; LW: 181

Mothering and writing. PHT: 136-138; YKW: 125

Others, what they think. RB: 195; CB: 102; JH: 172; CH: 163; ML: 202, 208; MM: 233; YKW: 122; LW: 176, 177, 178, 181

Publishing. CB: 105; JHH: 144-145, 146, 150; CH: 154, 162-163; ML: 202, 205; MM: 234; RV: 226; YKW: 123; LW: 176, 180, 181-182, 184

Silence. CB: 110; JHH: 142, 143; CH: 153, 164; ML: 203, 210; MM: 240-241 ; PHT: 132, 133-134; RV: 219-220; YKW: 114, 122; LW: 185

Sister. YKW: 114, 117, 120, 121

Sub-personalities. CH: 151-152, 159; JH: 171; ML: 200, 204, 206

Teachers. JH: 170; JHH: 142; ML: 202; MM: 237; PHT: 130; YKW: 117, 118; LW: 177

Voice, describe your writing. RB: 188; CB: 101-102; JH: 171-172; JHH: 139-140; CH: 151-152; ML: 199; MM: 231; PHT: 127, 128; RV: 213; YKW: 113

Work. RB: 189, 192; RV: 229; YKW: 123

Writer, identity as. RB: 188; CH: 163; ML: 202, 205, 207, 208, 211; MM: 236; RV: 221, 225; YKW: 113, 126; LW: 186

Writing, motivation. RB: 194; CB: 104-105, 107, 109; JH: 167; JHH: 145, 149; CH: 157-158; ML: 205; MM: 232, 234, 236, 244; RV: 222-223; YKW: 115, 123, 124; LW: 177-178, 179, 182

Writing, nemesis. CB: 111; CH: 164; JHH: 142; ML: 206; MM: 242; PHT: 134; RV: 223; YKW: 113-114, 124; LW: 184

Writing, process of. RB: 196-197; CB: 101, 104, 111; JH: 170-171; JHH: 147, 148, 149, 150; CH: 156, 161, 164, 165; ML: 199-200, 202-203, 204, 206; MM: 232, 233; PHT: 134-135; RV: 214, 216-217, 219, 222, 224, 226; YKW: 122, 123, 124; LW: 175, 179-180, 182, 183-184

Writing, schedule / discipline. RB: 196; JHH: 149; ML: 207; RV: 225; LW: 184-185